Between a Rock and
a Scarred Place

WITH LOVE AND
DEEP FRIENDSHIP

Between *a* Rock
and a
Scarred Place

*Relationship
Recovery for
Hurting
Hearts*

Jessica Lynn Taylor, Ph.D.

Just Living Today
Portland, Oregon

Between a Rock and a Scarred Place:
Relationship Recovery for Hurting Hearts

Copyright © 2013 Jessica Lynn Taylor

Published by Just Living Today, LLC
Portland, Oregon

Published in association with Coachzing Publishing
www.Coachzing.com

Cover and Interior Design: Joe Eckstein
Cover and Interior Photo: AlexMax/Bigstock.com

ISBN: 978-0-9911420-0-2

First Just Living Today printing: December 2013

Table of Contents

Part Two: Elevating the Conversation

Part Three: Overcoming Communication Challenges

Introduction

Thank you for taking a step of faith and picking up this book. I have some great news for you if you are looking to change the way that you live, love and interact with people in your life. You have just taken the first baby step that can lead to real heart and life change. Simply by looking for a way to better your communication and relationships, you have started a journey of growth. Congratulations on taking that first step!

In this book, you'll learn new skills that enable you to hear unspoken ideas behind spoken words, paving the way for greater understanding and strengthening your bonds with others.

We'll explore the connections and the communications that make up your life so you're better able to navigate your relationships.

For example, think about when a mother gives her child "the look." That child will stop dead in his tracks and know that his behavior modification skills better kick into high gear if he values his life. ***No words have to be exchanged for both parties to understand exactly what's going on.*** The connection that the mother and child share is deep enough that, in that moment, words aren't even necessary.

We're each hardwired to make connections with others. When relationships begin, we don't have to work very hard at connecting. It comes naturally. Most of us can find common ground, shared interests, and points of connection without digging too deep.

Why then is it so difficult to maintain and understand relationships?

As I began thinking about the concept of this book, I realized a common misperception about communication and relationships:

Connection with others is *not* the main issue. ***The ways in which we communicate are actually the primary causes of diminishing connections.*** As relationships progress, communication can get in the way of the connections that we once felt.

If we explore some primary human connections, we can see that the framework for connection with others is already laid:

- With a mother and baby, chemical bonds allow them to connect instantly. These chemical and psychological bonds are forming even before birth.

- In the beginning of a romantic courtship, most people with a connection feel they have endless things to talk about and an unquenchable curiosity about each other.

Have you ever felt a connection right away with someone? We feel connected when we feel understood and accepted. When we find that connection, we tend to want to hold onto it. These bonds that are formed in the beginning of a relationship are easy in their genesis, but far more difficult to maintain.

> *"The most important thing in communication is to hear what isn't being said."*
>
> **Peter F. Drucker**

Communication and Relationships

We tend to think that connection with someone else is the problem when things go wrong. When we do this, we're thinking about things in the wrong way. Our communication is what really keeps the connection alive. No amount of connection can keep a relationship together unless it's fostered with consistent, healthy communication.

The main factor in a loss of the initial connection is the loss of good communication and genuine interest in the other person and their needs.

At first, when things are new, we're extremely interested in discovering all the intricacies of another person or a new situation. As time goes by, however, we often become less and less interested in paying attention or becoming students of each other, and we become complacent. This is where we begin to feel that loss of connection.

This book explores how to communicate in ways that strengthen our connection with one another.

It details the importance of using communication for better living and will inspire you to think, reflect, and be the owner of your words, which will in turn help you to connect with others on a deeper level.

You'll discover how to get more of the connection you want in life by transcending the usual limits of communication.

As you put these practical and common sense solutions into practice, you'll find that your relationships are stronger than you ever thought possible.

Everything we discuss in this guide is a combination of my life experience, common sense, and the basic principle of reaping and sowing. I want to be clear up front that there is probably not an original thought in my head. Every word that I have ever read or written is a different combination of the same twenty-six letters. There is nothing magical about anything you will read in this book that will blow your mind or catapult you into the title of "relationship guru." It is the *consistent application* of simple truths that will change you and give you the confidence to heal your relationships and change your communications.

The key to deeper relationships through communication is the simple application of some highly effective techniques and a dedication to change.

In the pursuit of continued connection, you'll learn how to elevate your day-to-day conversations with your spouse, children, family, friends and co-workers. You can develop this connection by taking advantage of the power of your words, implementing effective listening techniques, and mastering strategies of searching for meaning.

In this practical system of communication, you'll learn to search for authentic meaning and assign values to the messages others send you through their words, tone, requests and actions.

I have been using these methods in my own relationships. As a result, I have found a deep level of relational fulfillment. My experience is a journey that I'm still on: I want to find more effective ways to connect at a deeper level to the people I love.

Nothing that is written in this book is being touted as a new concept. It's often easy to forget the practical wisdom of common sense thinking. Rediscovering these basics in an applicable manner will be more life altering than any new age technique you try.

These concepts are simple but their application is a stumbling block for so many. I'm here to help guide you in this process of growth as you apply these principles to your life. I will share what I have learned about connecting with others in the hope that people like you, who seek to deepen your relationships, will be able to enhance the ways you learn, love, listen and communicate.

I'm passionate about helping others apply these concepts in ways that strengthen families, communities, and relationships.

> *"The three great essentials to achieve anything worthwhile are, first, hard work; second, stick-to-itiveness; third, common sense."*
>
> **Thomas A. Edison**

Why Do We Need This Book?

The concept for this book came out of the dysfunction that I have enabled in my life. It came from my failures and struggles to connect. Talk about writing a *self-help* book! This concept came from the idea that I needed to genuinely implement better communication before I could coach, teach and inspire others to do the same. I realized that I needed to write a book to read over and over when I forget how to function well in my relationships. This writing is as much for me as for you.

When I realized that I was not alone in my struggle for better connections, I took a leap of faith and decided to share my mess with others. This writing is from my heart and from the lessons I have learned. I warn you that it will not always be pretty or flattering to see my colossal failures, but I hope that it can inspire you to keep trying.

I see a need for people to connect and come to an understanding of each other. This need is at the foundation of most issues now and from the dawn of time. Our government systems, our family system, and relationships in general suffer from a lack of communication and understanding.

This book assists families and individuals to rethink their communication styles as they strive for greater connection.

I want to encourage people to communicate with others on a deeper level, through intentional questioning, simple language changes, and values-driven conversations.

We can accomplish this not through new communication tricks or fancy jargon, but through exploring the depths of both those we love and ourselves. We do this in order to connect in heartfelt and meaningful ways to the people we care for, but sometimes struggle to understand.

In this book we will work together to elevate the words and intentions of conversations to bring about healing and growth in your relationships.

Without relationships, life is vacant and futile. **We're created to love and be loved.** When we deny this fact, chaos in government, families and life ensues. Picking up this book suggests that at some level you understand the foundational nature of relationships and their role in whole life fulfillment.

> *"Life is relationships; the rest is just details."*
>
> **Gary Smalley**

Who Will This Book Serve?

If you're alive and breathing, you will certainly encounter other people. If you've found a way to disappear and avoid all human connection, please share with the rest of us so that from time to time we can take a much-needed vacation from others.

Relationships and life are difficult to navigate. The great thing is that right now I have a choice in what I do. Life is a gift and I plan to unwrap it and treasure it with all of the people that I love to the best of my ability.

A mentor of mine lives by the motto "Loving people, because people matter." That pretty much sums it up for me. People and relationships matter and it's to my highest benefit to explore how to connect with others in a meaningful way.

This book has the possibility to inspire people at any age, stage or circumstance in life. If you understand that relationships matter more than all of the technical details of life, you're getting off to a great start.

As long as you're currently navigating life with others, the tools in this book can be life-giving to your relationships.

You might find this content especially interesting and helpful if you're:

* a pastor or lay leader
* a teacher or other educator
* a counselor or coach in the relationship or communication field
* a parent or teen who is feeling disconnected
* a community service partner or service-based business owner
* in a romantic relationship and looking for a deeper connection
* struggling to be understood or to understand others
* seeking connection with the people around you

Our relationships with others are of paramount importance. All of the other things in life are meaningless unless we have people to share them with. As we explore our relationships, we want to put them above all of the details and make them our primary focus. Changing the details is one thing, but changing your relationships changes your life.

> *"Our greatest fear as individuals . . . should not be of failure but of succeeding at things in life that don't really matter."*
>
> **Francis Chan,** *Crazy Love*

What Problems Does This Book Address?

I grew up hearing that if I wanted to learn patience, it would only come through being given things to wait for. We have all had the pleasure of being taught patience through learning to deal with difficult people. This book helps to address how to take responsibility for what is yours and leave the rest.

We'll learn to combat merely *reacting* to others by learning how to *respond* to others in ways that can deepen our relationship instead of destroy it.

We will look at some of the most pressing and common relationship challenges in ways that will help you apply new techniques to your unique situation.

Have you ever asked yourself questions like these?

- Why is it so hard for people to understand me?

- I'm so frustrated. I just don't understand my _____ (spouse, kids, friend).

- How can I communicate better if the other person has completely shut down or is emotionally dead?

- I have no common ground to stand on with the person I'm talking with. Where do we even start?

- What if I try and the other person rejects my efforts?

- I cannot be emotionally vulnerable anymore. I have been hurt too many times. How could I ever trust again?

- How do I balance being honest while still being sensitive to the feelings of another person?

- I need to draw some boundaries for healthy communication, but I don't know how or even where to start.

- How do I insist on being treated kindly and spoken to respectfully with people who refuse to do that?

- How do I know if a relationship is worth salvaging after so many failed attempts?

- How do I address the manipulation that is used in so many of my relationships?

- What am I responsible for in my relationships?

- Do I always have to be the one to change and make the effort?

This book will teach you ways to overcome situations like these and turn them into positive opportunities to strengthen your relationships. Hopefully you will learn how to better love and understand yourself and others in dynamic ways.

> *"Love doesn't erase the past, but it makes the future different."*
>
> **Gary Chapman**, *The 5 Love Languages Singles Edition*

Part One:

Laying the Groundwork

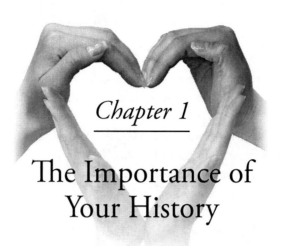

Chapter 1

The Importance of Your History

Before beginning any project, it is wise to lay a solid foundation. Putting in the hard work up front helps ensure that the final product of your efforts is something that will last. This is the reason researching your past is such an important part of this life changing work. I will be the first to admit that exploring my history is not high on my "would love to do today" list. For many, the traditions passed down from their families are not conducive to building deep relationships. Maybe your life lessons came in the form of "Thanks Mom and Dad. That is what *not* to do with my life."

However, regardless of your family of origin issues, your past is the key to unlocking how you became the person you are now.

Your past plays a critical role in how you communicate, connect with others, and form relationships. Luckily, though, your past does *not* have to define your future. Balancing these forces helps us to see that the past is valuable for informing our future, although it does not have to shape it.

One of the biggest choices you'll ever make is the choice of how to view your past. ***You can be a slave and a product of your past or you can choose to use it as a launching place for the future you desire.***

Making the choice to move forward from your past comes with its own set of complications, but it's a far more worthy venture than living as you've always lived and getting the same results.

As we move through issues of our past, it's not as simple as replacing behaviors. We need to go deeper into what is behind our behavior and the underlying assumptions and beliefs that influenced the behavior in the first place.

It is crucial to develop a drive to go in an intentional direction with your life purpose. Without this pointed direction to our lives, we tend to float along with the currents of where circumstances lead us. Sometimes setting this intentional path means doing the exact opposite of what feels normal.

Family of Origin Issues and Family Dynamics

We must explore where we're coming from before we understand where we're capable of going. When we look at how the people in our lives have influenced us, we can gain insight into why we have become who we are now.

It's helpful to look at the people in your life who had the *biggest* influences, both positive and negative. Then, you can consciously extract the qualities you admire and leave behind the qualities you find to be less desirable.

This is not about placing blame or being critical. It's all about taking an inventory of what we were each given to work with.

When we understand the influence of the past, we can make intentional choices about what works for us and what doesn't.

As an adult, we're completely responsible for our own choices. We select our path and the attitudes we want to include in our lives. You might have been running on autopilot until this point, but now it's time to take on the task of thoughtfully and deliberately making choices.

The realization that life is about choices is radical for many people. In taking responsibility for our lives and relationships, we see that everything boils down to the choices that we make.

You may be reading this and thinking, "Well, I've decided that I will not make intentional choices so I won't have to take responsibility for my life or actions." However, if you think you're off the hook, please understand that a lack of willingness to make a choice is, in and of itself, a choice!

We get to choose our words, actions, attitudes, and growth despite our circumstances.

We can all fall into the trap of believing that wanting something to happen is the same as actually making it happen. I am sorry to tell you, friend, these things are not the same.

For instance, I once asked my mother about her childhood parenting beliefs. What kind of parent did she aspire to be? I had to choke back laughter when I heard her response. She said that she had vowed to be nothing like her own mother and that she would never tell her children the word "No." She believed she would always be able to find a more positive answer.

Now, let's all take a moment and laugh.

This might have been her original intention, but it didn't become a reality in my childhood. In fact, I'm glad that she changed her mind and learned the power of the word "No." This word taught me boundaries, kept me from danger, and helped me learn the discipline of patience.

My mother changed her thinking as she gained more parenting and life experience of her own. She didn't reach her original ideals, but made new ones with the wisdom that came from experience.

We can do the same. This takes a desire to make choices based on the new information that we gain through our life experiences.

As we gain new information and experiences, we can learn to change our original thinking in order to develop a habit or action that serves us better.

We have to let go of both the issues of our upbringing and the expectations we placed on ourselves rooted in our naïve thoughts about who we wanted to become.

For you, this may be as simple as making a single choice or it may be the beginning of a long, complex, healing journey. The more childhood issues that are left unresolved, the more relational issues you'll experience as an adult.

When we attend to issues that are difficult and painful, we give ourselves the opportunity for advancement from the experiences, instead of allowing the experiences to inhibit our growth permanently.

I'm not suggesting that we spend time wallowing in the past, but to move to the future we need to work through the tribulations of the past that have the potential to hinder our progress.

It's a wise practice to learn to identify the barriers that you might face and then move ahead with a plan for navigating those barriers.

When we start to examine and evaluate our past, instead of just saying, "All of my struggles define me," we can say, "These are the things that have become stepping stones for my growth. These are the challenges that I have been able to move past, and that have made me who I am."

Dealing with these issues allows you to create new relationships that aren't based on the old patterns of dysfunction that may be comfortable for you.

Such influences from your past, left unexamined, can complicate your current relationships, stifle connection with others, and prevent communicating effectively.

Don't try to skip this step in your process! Take the time to become a student of yourself and your life story. Once you have a grip on your past and present, you can move confidently into your future.

This work is not only crucial for self-development, but also for forming healthy relationships. It's important to recognize our current patterns and be open about ourselves before we can expect others to be transparent with us.

> *"Letting go means to come to the realization that some people are a part of your history, but not a part of your destiny."*
>
> **Steve Maraboli**, *Unapologetically You: Reflections on Life and the Human Experience*

Chapter 2

How Have Our Communications Evolved to Where They Are Today?

Our childhood communication styles and presumptions can create a pattern for the rest of our lives. We must examine these dynamics and take inventory of what works in our current context and what is destructive.

As a child I thought that the best form of communication was yelling. This wasn't yelling just to be mean. It served a practical purpose. Living in a larger family, we learned to cope with lots of people and noise. If you could pause the interactions of my childhood at any given moment, you might see that everyone in the picture has their mouths open.

There was plenty of talking, but no communication.

It takes both a speaker and a listener to hold a conversation. In my family, there were lots of mouths but very few ears.

As I examined my childhood, I realized I had learned some unhealthy messages about volume. The message I took away was, "*Whoever is the loudest is the rightest.*" This was fostered in knowing that unless I was loud, I literally would not be heard.

Unfortunately, I also learned that if I talked over someone or yelled, I somehow "won" the conversation because I forced him or her to "hear" me.

We all know that although we may be talking, it's possible that we're not being heard. I had to learn that this type of behavior, although understandable due to circumstance, would not serve me well.

As an adult with mature relationships, I had to realize that my tone of voice, volume, and words *all* had an effect on how people viewed me, how I came across, and how people felt about their relationships with me.

My dysfunctional way of yelling to get my point across might have worked in my old context, but in the adult world I found that it was less than effective.

For example, how many of us were told as children, "Go find your brothers and sisters and tell them it's time for dinner?" This is a fairly common experience.

When I was asked to gather the family for dinner, I was usually too absorbed in myself to do this effectively. As you may have guessed, much to the displeasure of my parents, this usually induced a loud bellowing of "Dinner!" in the general geographical location of my siblings.

This technique was hardly helpful or effective. What my parents wanted was for me to go find everyone and let them know that dinner was ready. What they got was more noise and yet another shot at practicing patience with a teenager.

Now imagine that I never chose to change that behavior. I'm now an adult sitting at work when my boss asks me to relay information to my team. I proceed to stand on my desk and announce, "Boss has some stuff for us to go over" to the team at all ends of the building. This is obviously not effective or what my boss was trying to get me to do.

Now, other than the obvious job loss in my future, I have some other important issues to address as well.

Instead of holding onto yelling and being disengaged in the process of communication, I needed to change my methods. I had to learn how to be more articulate and appropriate, not just louder.

This revelation helped me to develop my communication skills within relationships in my adult context.

The path of least resistance is easier, but it's not necessarily better.

You may think to yourself, "Why should we address these issues? Isn't it easier to keep going how we have always gone? Even if my way is not the most effective, it's what I'm comfortable doing."

We all know that when we're doing what we've always done, we will continue getting what we've always gotten. ***Are you content with your relationship results, or would you welcome a change?***

When we face the past, we're ready to develop from it and move into the future. Our past contributes to who we are, but it doesn't necessarily dictate who we have to become.

> *"You are not a victim. No matter what you have been through, you're still here. You may have been challenged, hurt, betrayed, beaten, and discouraged, but nothing has defeated you. You are still here! You have been delayed but not denied. You are not a victim, you are a victor. You have a history of victory."*
>
> **Steve Maraboli**, *Unapologetically You: Reflections on Life and the Human Experience*

Chapter 3

Communicating Your Love

F or some people, if I asked them to describe their relationships in terms of a garden, they might paint a less than wonderful picture. "Well, here are all the thorns, there is a rotting pile of compost over there, and there is a giant load of manure over there!" Many of us have untended "relationship gardens" that are a mess.

You may see only a manure pile in your relationships right now, but guess what? That manure is the perfect fertilizer to spur something beautiful to grow. It will stink and be messy, but the payoff is well worth the work.

When you can most effectively communicate your love, you cultivate a garden of commitment and joy for yourself and those you love.

Relationships Are Like a Garden

When we sow seeds, we can only expect to reap the fruit of what we actually put in the ground.

Many times, when you look at your relationships and communication, it's helpful to ask yourself, *"What am I sowing into my relationships?"* If I'm constantly sowing dissention, anger and judgment, I shouldn't expect to have a loving relationship blossom.

As the gardener of my relationships, I get to decide what goes in. This means that I have influence in what comes out and the quality of the fruit I produce. If I sow seeds that don't have deep roots and give them limited care, those seeds aren't going to bear the same fruit as something that I cultivate and care for deeply.

Have you prepared the soil of your life to bear good relational fruit and are you willing to put in the work to create something living, growing and sustainable?

Does this mean that each and every relationship will be a huge amount of work? Luckily, not every relationship takes this amount of effort. Some relationships are more like grass. They need limited attention. The relationships that are most important to you are the ones to focus this "gardener's" energy on.

We can have lots of surface level relationships where we're content to be courteous and kind but the goal is not growth.

However, the relationships at home need to be cultivated with love so that they can bear genuinely satisfying fruit.

> *"Human beings, like plants, grow in the soil of acceptance, not in the atmosphere of rejection."*
>
> **John Powell**

The 5 Love Languages

In school, most students are required to take classes in a second language. This is not merely for the sake of torture, as some students may feel, but for the sake of growth. Learning another language expands the brain and allows for better critical thinking skills. It allows us to explore other cultures and it can even be beneficial in helping us to understand our native language better.

It would have been wonderful if I had used my language classes to learn these valuable lessons. Instead, I chose to use learning another language to my advantage in another way.

When I was in high school, I loved speaking Spanish. This did not come from a love of the language, but a love of being able to speak so some people around me couldn't understand me. It was a much more effective code language than "Pig Latin!"

This coded language was entertaining because I could bash the curriculum or express my disdain for the teacher openly without repercussion, that is, until the day I did this in Spanish class.

My desk partner, who is still a great friend of mine, was mortified when one day I began a rant in my "code language," including very specific and strong words about my loathing of the class. I continued on and on, not understanding the concerned look on my friend's face.

It was not until the teacher had tilted her head to the side and widened her eyes that I made the connection. This "code" I was speaking was the native tongue of my teacher and she had heard and understood every word.

She must have figured that my idiotic behavior was punishment enough because she walked away and smiled as my friend burst into laughter.

To this day, I think often about this incident and am reminded of my own narrow thinking. I no longer use Spanish as a code language and I stick to proving my lesser intelligence in my native language.

This life lesson on languages did broaden my perspective, though, and helped me realize how important language is in relationships and communication.

In my pursuit of deeper, more meaningful relationships, I read Gary Chapman's book, *The 5 Love Languages*. As I studied the concepts in this book, my thinking about relationships was completely transformed.

He explains how ***we each have a specific way we desire to be loved.*** With this understanding of the special nature of love, we can draw the conclusion that there are special ways to communicate with others so they can experience our love for them more fully.

When we think about relationship communication in terms of languages, this concept can begin to make more sense. We can be on the same page if we learn to speak the language of others.

Many of us are selfish in our thinking of languages. Perhaps you wonder, "Why should I have to learn the language of another person?"

In truth, you don't have to. But when you make the choice to learn someone else's language, you're making communication more effective for *both* of you.

In learning these other relational languages, you make your life easier and ensure that when you speak, others can understand and take to heart what you say.

We've all seen how communication can break down when two people don't share a common language. Many people talk louder, slower, or use exaggerated gestures to get their point across in a situation like this. However, if someone cannot understand your language, no matter how loud or long you talk, you won't make your point.

Are you speaking in a relational language that others understand?

Taking these concepts to heart was a starting point in growth for my conversations and connections. Once I became a student of my family and other close relationships, I was able to see how to better connect with them.

I was no longer just speaking louder, hoping to be heard. Instead, I began learning the preferred love language of my heart and the hearts of those around me so that I could better understand how to communicate my love. I struggled through speaking in their language so they could understand me.

You'll find that others don't care much about the structure of your language or speaking skills. They just want to see that you're willing to try to speak in a way that they can understand.

This can be a powerful shift in thinking as you realize that relationships are not all about talking, but rather about *effectively* communicating.

According to Gary Chapman, the 5 love languages are:

* Quality Time
* Acts of Service
* Gifts
* Words of Affirmation
* Physical Touch

Even though all these languages are pleasant to us, only one or two of them speak deeply to the core of who we are as a person.

Let's look closer at the details of each love language:

1. **Quality Time.** Quality time has to do with eye contact and one-on-one face time with the other person in a relationship. It's important for that time to be uninterrupted, unplugged, and intentional.

   If this is your primary love language, your most satisfying times—the times in which you feel most loved and connected—are the times when you spend quality time with someone.

   The key concept is quality. You may have spent two hours watching a movie with a friend, but for a person who speaks this language, they would need to engage in connection and conversation after the movie to feel fulfilled with the interaction.

2. **Acts of Service.** You might value this love language the most if you feel loved when someone does something especially for you.

   In communicating to a person with this love language, your act could be as simple as switching over the laundry, making dinner, or doing something you know they would enjoy.

   The Acts of Service language speaks to those who are action-oriented and need to see by your actions that you love them.

3. **Gifts.** Gift giving is important to those who really love to give and receive items.

   You can show your love to them even with inexpensive or homemade gifts. Small gifts, cards, or trinkets act as physical signs of affection towards those with this primary love language.

   They would be thrilled to hear you say, "I went to the beach and found this shell. It reminded me of you," or, "I saw this at the grocery store and I knew it was your favorite snack so I picked it up." Gift givers often demonstrate their love in this same way.

4. **Words of Affirmation.** If you value the Words of Affirmation language, you can be deeply touched by the words of others. It's important for you to be told "Thank you," "I love you" and "That was a great thing you did."

   You need those words from others to affirm you, and that verbal message is what really warms your heart.

5. **Physical Touch.** This language is defined as a non-sexual physical touch. The person who speaks this language feels really loved when you hold their hand, give them a hug, or sit close to them.

Physical interaction is what they desire. They love to cuddle, wrestle, play, and be in close proximity to those they care about.

This may scare some people who don't like their personal space invaded, but for those who speak this language, there is no better way to show your love.

As we learn and explore our primary languages, we can begin to see which of our relational needs are being met. Looking at the specific categories can help us as we seek to understand others and how they feel loved.

For example, let's say someone who is "Quality Time" is talking to someone who is "Physical Touch:"

Mr. "Physical Touch" just wants a hug to feel connected.

In the meantime, Mr. "Quality Time" is starting into a lengthy conversation about his life. Mr. "Quality Time" gives Mr. "Physical Touch" a cold handshake and continues on with his conversation.

Mr. "Physical Touch" feels dejected and mentally checks out of the conversation.

In this interaction, neither person got his needs met and there was an awkward exchange that resulted in both parties walking away feeling unfulfilled.

Understanding these principles can help eliminate so much confusion and relational misunderstanding.

Realizing that how you feel love isn't always how another person feels love is useful for deepening your relationships. When we consider another person's love language and learn how they can best be loved, we show an immense interest and care for their needs. What is more endearing than that?

Try these approaches to determine the love language of others:

1. **Ask them.** Sometimes, the best way to find out another person's love language is to present the five languages to them and ask them what stands out.

   If they give you an answer along the lines of, "I like all of them," explain how one or two will really speak to their heart more than the others. If they lived without one particular expression, they would feel extremely unloved.

   They can start going through the list individually and asking, "Well, if somebody didn't give me a gift, would that upset me? No. If somebody didn't affirm me in their words, would that upset me? No." That way, they can narrow down the list to the love language that rings true for them.

   Go through the list with them and start checking off the things that are non-essential to making them feel deeply loved. Then all you're left with are the languages that mean the most to them.

2. **Observe which language they speak.** You can become an observer of the other person. ***Frequently, but not always, people speak and love to be spoken to in the same language.*** Be an observer of the actions of others.

   If someone is known for making something or giving you a gift, you might think, "Maybe they're a person whose primary language is gift giving. I can try to respond to them in that manner." Try not to assume as you're doing this.

   Sometimes it's clear and other times it's not. When in doubt, ask them. I don't know very many people that would be enraged if you requested to know how to love them more effectively!

3. **Notice when they express gratitude.** If your loved one is extremely grateful that you came to visit, had coffee with them, and spent an hour chatting with them, they may value the Quality Time language. Look at what the people around you tend to appreciate.

   As we become students of each other, we can learn each other's love languages.
   When we deliberately engage and discover how to love and respect others, relationships become more fulfilling for both parties. This type of love is grounded in respect for the

other person. It honors others above the self and acknowledges that each person is unique and has specific needs.

> *"Respect begins with this attitude: 'I acknowledge that you're a creature of extreme worth . . . I will seek to understand you and grant you the freedom to think differently from the way I think and to experience emotions that I may not experience.' Respect means that you give the other person the freedom to be an individual."*
>
> **Gary Chapman,** *The 5 Love Languages*

Chapter 4

Determining the Purpose of Each Conversation

In order to get the greatest benefit from this book and its concepts, it's vital to first determine the purpose of your communications with others. When you determine the purpose of the conversation, you can be better prepared to communicate in a meaningful manner.

Sometimes communication is transactional in nature, which would mean you're giving or receiving basic information without any deeper meaning attached.

When a relationship needs this type of communication, you don't need to go deeper by using the more advanced skills you'll find here. Surface level communication is appropriate.

Surface Level Conversations

Surface level conversations could happen with a neighbor you pass by on a walk or the server at a restaurant. These are the folks that you run into in everyday life. You're just going to answer their question. There's no deeper meaning assigned to their words or the communication.

For example, think about the barista at the coffee shop. She might ask you, "Is there anything else I can do for you today?"

This is not the time to hand her a list of life goals that you think she might like to hear about in detail. This shows a lack of understanding on your part. Her question was transactional. Even the nature of her relationship with you is transactional. Your conversations can be fun and polite, but they don't need to be developed at a deeper level in all cases.

In these situations, you can ask yourself, "Are they being polite but also transactional?" After you've made this assessment, you can know where to begin and end the connection.

This doesn't mean that transactional relationships aren't important. However, focusing your energy on your surface level connections will become tiresome and unfulfilling.

These connections don't need to be stressful. Know that some people are those that you choose to invest in and "do life with." Other people are those who are "doing life around you." It's important to understand the difference.

> *"I'm very careful to be shallow and conventional where depth and originality are wasted."*
>
> **L.M. Montgomery**

Deeper Conversations

When someone shows genuine concern, they're diving into a deeper form of communication. This concern is often made evident by the speaker using elevated questioning. This is when a friend might see that you look sad and ask you, "What's going on?" You know they're actually concerned and it's time for an answer with more depth than, "Nothing" or "I'm Okay."

They're asking a deeper question that has meaning attached and expecting to hear a meaningful answer. It will help you communicate more effectively if you learn to identify the difference between people in your life that actually want to know the answer to these questions and those that ask out of courtesy or obligation.

Sometimes we try to hide our feelings when someone asks because we fear that they don't care, or we don't want to burden them with our struggle. In hiding our feelings, though, we send mixed messages. At times, it's clear that something is wrong but we're unwilling to engage the other person in our hurt.

This could happen when you ask somebody, "How are you doing?" and they say "Fine," when you can obviously tell they're not having a great day.

Be careful if you're often cryptic like this in your answers. You run the risk of isolating yourself from those who care about you:

* Some people will begin to take your assurance of being "fine" at face value.
* Others can be hurt and think you don't trust them with your real feelings.
* They might get tired of trying to decode your pain and give up asking altogether.
* Some will wonder if you're seeking attention rather than connection.

Relationship breakdown happens when we communicate cryptically with one another and expect the other person in the relationship to decode our emotional message.

When Should You Go Deeper? When Should You Stay on the Surface?

As you're starting to communicate more effectively, determining the level of communication can be a powerful skill. Understanding the purposes and reasoning behind a conversation can help you decipher when to go deeper and when to stay on the surface.

Looking at your own skin can bring great clarity to this concept:

The outer layer of your skin is meant to protect you. It's waterproof and keeps disease and bacteria out. It mainly serves as a cover over all of the more complex processes that are going on in your body underneath the skin.

You can look at some of your relationships or surface level conversations like the outer layer of your skin. Some things are just meant to be informational, or to get us to the next stage. They are not deeper issues. Think of these as your surface relationships. They serve a purpose but they're only one layer.

For example, if you're asking your child what they would like for dinner, you're asking for specific information. ***This is a transactional issue*** for the purpose of communicating information.

When we can learn to differentiate these issues from deeper ones, we can save ourselves the effort of worrying and reading something deeper into communications with little value.

The first step in elevating your conversations is to determine what the person is trying to communicate.

- Are they giving or asking for information?
- Are they asking a simple question?
- Is this a surface issue, or is this a deeper issue?

When you're able to make this determination, you'll feel more connected with those you love.

You'll also avoid conflict that can come along with relational interactions, such as when one person is trying to obtain information and the other person is trying to assign or extract a deeper meaning. In the end, neither receives what they need.

With a little practice, you can determine situations in which it's to your benefit to elevate a conversation. Now you're ready to learn how to make that transition to the next stage.

"The search for meaning in our lives takes us on paths large and small. When we go beyond ourselves—whether in forgiveness, unselfishness, thoughtfulness, generosity and understanding toward others—we enter into the spiritual realm of meaning. By giving beyond ourselves, we make our own lives richer. This is a truth long understood at the heart of all meaningful spiritual traditions. It's a mystery that can only be experienced. And when we do experience it, we're in the heart of meaning."

Alex Pattakos, *Prisoners of Our Thoughts: Viktor Frankl's Principles for Discovering Meaning in Life and Work*

Action Steps for Higher Function

Imagine climbing a mountain. As you climb, your legs may get tired and your ears might pop uncomfortably as they adjust to the higher elevation. There can be a change in your breathing as the air thins. You might even begin to feel light headed. All of these things may happen as you exert yourself in the effort to reach the top.

The most amazing part of the whole experience, even with all of the pain, is when you turn around and look at the view. ***Your perspective at an elevated point is expanded to include so much more than when you began your journey.***

Elevating your relationships and conversations is the same concept. You'll enjoy opening your mind to higher level functioning and making a serious effort to raise the bar for your communication. It's hard work to continue taking step after step, but the payoff is a whole new perspective.

Use this acronym to ELEVATE your conversations in seven steps:

E: Enter without judgment

L: Listen with intention

E: Engage with open-ended questions

V: Visit the other person's perspective

A: Ask for permission and clarification

T: Take away meaning, not just content

E: Extend an invitation for deeper connection, with gratitude

1. **Enter the conversation without judgment.** Instead of coming in with a preconceived notion of how someone might react or what the outcome of the conversation might be, the first step to elevating your connection is leaving that judgment out of the conversation until you have more information.

2. **Listen with intention.** Listen to the words of the other person and then think about the things they might be implying. You're still not making a judgment or assessment, but intentionally listening for meaning.

3. **Engage with open-ended questions.** Try to gain insight into the other person by opening up the question to longer answers than just "yes" or "no." Ask "why" or "how" questions.

4. **Visit the other person's perspective.** Step into their shoes and ask yourself, "How do they see things? How might they feel in this conversation?" *This is critical as you elevate the connection* because you're bringing their feelings into the conversation as an integral piece.

5. **Ask for permission and clarification.** Avoid assumptions. Ask for permission to reflect. Ask questions to clarify meaning if it seems unclear.

6. **Take away meaning, not just content.** After you've clarified what they're saying, look for meaning and values, not just the actual words spoken.

When you're able to take away meaning with the words, you tap into a deeper level of communicating. It's not just about facts, but also their perspective, feelings, and reflections on the topic.

This process helps you raise the conversation to a higher level: instead of just being a transactional exchange of information, you're now exchanging meaning and values.

7. **Extend an invitation for a deeper connection, with gratitude.** *The key is "with gratitude."* You want to help the conversation continue by following these steps and then thank the person for sharing with you.

This helps them feel heard and valued and it makes for better and easier communication the next time.

One of the biggest challenges to using these tools is the fact that it's much easier to go about life not elevating our conversations. Just exchanging information, talking to be heard, or listening for content is how most of us communicate on a regular basis.

You'll most likely need to shift your habits to intentionally raise the conversation to a different level. This takes practice, time, and dedication.

The best way to overcome this challenge is to remember that the end result is better, deeper communication with the people you care about. Also, you can use these skills to become an excellent communicator. You can become somebody that others will love to talk with, open up to, and share deeply with.

It's a great feeling to know you can truly be there for others—not only in your words, but also through your actions.

You can also forge a deeper connection in the way you respond to conflict.

Responding to Conflict

Much of the time when conflict arises, my first instinct is to respond with "Oh no you didn't!" The problem with this statement is that, almost without fail, the person did in fact do or say something that is upsetting to me. This reaction is not helpful, nor does it make sense.

If you recognize this same type of reaction in your responses, it would serve you better to elevate the conversation instead.

Remind yourself: "I'm responsible for how I respond. When I pause and think before I respond, I can ensure that my words convey what I need them to while at the same time enabling a deeper connection to take place."

As we know, conversations work in a cyclical manner. One person speaks and the other person responds. Once you have elevated the conversation and the other person has responded, it's imperative that you direct the communication in a constructive manner.

This acronym will help you get to a deeper connection with your responses:

REPLY:

Is it	**R**easonable in nature?
Are my	**E**motions balanced?
Is my	**P**assion realized?
Did I	**L**isten fully?
Did I	**Y**ield to the best of the other person?

It's easy to jump straight into making a quick retort to someone else's criticism, clarifying question, or inquiry. However, if you pause just for a moment, you can differentiate between your "head reply" and your "mouth reply."

Your "head reply" may begin with "Oh girl" and it can easily spiral into a "You don't know me" or back to the notorious "Oh no you didn't!" These types of responses only serve to continue a negative cycle of communication which really drives you apart instead of bringing you closer together.

On the other hand, when you ask yourself the following questions before you reply, you elevate the conversation to a level where you're accountable for the things you say. This is where your "head reply" is changed to your "mouth reply."

When you formulate your reply, ask yourself these questions:

- **Is it reasonable in nature?** Is my reply something I would be proud of and that is a reasonable thing to say at the time? Have I blown things out of proportion or taken things out of context?

- **Are my emotions balanced?** Am I extremely angry, sad, or hurt? If the answer is yes, your replies could be emotional, rash and detrimental to your relationship.

- **Is my passion realized?** Are the things I'm passionate about demonstrated in this reply? Just because we're keeping our emotions under control and ensuring we're accountable doesn't mean we need to leave our passion, heart and values at the door. We need to express these appropriately.

- **Did I listen fully?** Before you reply, it's important you understand fully what you're replying to. When you've listened fully, you can then reply with confidence.

- **Did I yield to the best of the other person?** Did I stop and think about the other person above myself before my reply? ***This is probably the most crucial step,*** because it allows you to avoid saying things that are hurtful, that you'll have to apologize for later, or that you'll regret. It shows you truly value the other person.

If you're struggling to figure out what might be reasonable, test yourself by gauging the tone of the

conversation. If the other person is very calm and suddenly you're exploding, that doesn't seem like a reasonable response. Conversely, if the other person is explosive, you hopefully understand it's not a reasonable response or an attitude you should reflect.

This is where you look around and evaluate the circumstances: the tone of voice being used, as well as the importance of the issue. Then you can decide if what you have to say is reasonable or if it's rash or hurtful.

As we value others in our conversations, we also value ourselves. Are you connecting to what's important to you? Why is it important? These questions refer to your own values.

These techniques enable you to passionately let people know how you're feeling and what's going on in your life, in a way they can connect with.

Passion reflects what you value. ***Your conversations should reveal the things that are true for you, important to you, and crucial to your character.*** These values define who you are and how you function in the world. As you're able to move into action with your values, your life and relationships will flourish.

For example, if you value love and understanding, you want to make sure that as your passion is being realized, you're letting others see that you're coming from a place of love and understanding, not just from a place of anger or eagerness to get your point across.

With these new tools in place, you're now ready to move forward in the process. Remember that all of these tools are useful for practical application, but an unchanged heart and mind will not apply even the most genius of principles.

Prepare yourself to be changed so that the application of these concepts can have a lasting and genuine impact on your relationships.

An internal change causes the outer transformation that triggers others to take notice. This process of self-renovation is precisely the process that has the power to change the world from the inside out. No external pressure could ever be as powerful as someone who has chosen to truly transform themselves.

You have now laid the groundwork and foundation for change. Let's get to work.

> *"What we can and should change is ourselves: our impatience, our egoism (including intellectual egoism), our sense of injury, our lack of love and forbearance. I regard every other attempt to change the world, even if it springs from the best intentions, as futile."*
>
> **Hermann Hesse**

Part Two:

Elevating the
Conversation

Chapter 5

Preparing for Life-Changing Communication

What is it costing you to continue down your relational paths as they are now?

In my own life, I have come to see that before I'm actually willing to change, I have to recognize the pain that is caused by my inaction. I could give you a thousand examples of times when I was unwilling to change my behavior even though I had all the information I needed. It took feeling the pain of *not* changing to convince me to take action toward change.

We all seem to resist change, even when we know it's for our ultimate good and benefit. However, when you pair information with inspiration, you have the magic formula that provides the real motivation to change.

Sometimes this inspiration has to come with hitting rock bottom or a place where hope feels lost.

We prefer to stay in our comfort zone, even when that comfort zone is a path of destruction and leaves us unhealthy and fighting consequences.

For example, one of the biggest changes I've made in my life has been taking control of my health. Through ignoring my feelings and overeating, I found myself at a dangerous weight. It wasn't until I was in such a poor state of health that I realized my actions had extremely negative consequences in my life.

I also realized that I was literally putting a barrier around me to distance myself from people. I was filling myself with food instead of good relationships with deep connections. I was substituting fulfilling relationships with filling my stomach.

It wasn't until I got to that point where I was physically hurting and in danger that the consequences of my actions dawned on me. I knew all along that I was not making healthy choices, but until I arrived at a place of ruin, I was not willing to do the hard work to alter my heart or behavior.

We all have a breaking point. It's different for each of us, but we have to get to the point where we realize that what we're doing no longer works.

My prayer for you is that you don't have to get to a traumatic point in your relationships before you decide to take the first steps toward changing.

The fact that you're reading this reflects that you have the desire for healthy relationships. Unfortunately, this desire alone is not enough. You can read everything in this book and in every book ever written, but without the motivation that leads to action, successful change will be long in coming.

So how can you gain the motivation you need to take action in areas where you know transformation is needed?

There are two ways:

1. **Make the conscious decision to change yourself.** You can even do it little by little, one small step at a time, but you're still taking action to move forward toward the life you truly desire.

2. **Wait until circumstances come into your life that force change upon you.** This severely limits your options and makes change come as a result of necessity and not a desire to transform.

When Should You Begin?

For your best results, the perfect time to begin is now. We're not guaranteed even our next breath, so take advantage of the life you're given and take action!

Sometimes, it might take getting to your breaking point for you to decide that it's worth the pain and challenge of going through a change. But at least this is where you'll see the light at the end of the tunnel. When your thinking shifts in this area, you realize that the pain of not changing or doing nothing is actually worse than the pain it will take to transform.

Don't wait until you're in the middle of a divorce, in relationship turmoil, or at the tipping point of severing ties to start the process of change!

When is it that couples start going to marriage counseling? It's usually after a big fight, infidelity, crisis, or a breakdown. However, relational decline actually happens over time. There is a slow decay that eventually leads to a problem big enough to get the attention of one or both partners.

I had a wonderful professor in college who confided in our class that he had been married for many years and had been in marriage counseling the whole time. Most students expected him to talk about how horrible this marriage was because it required perpetual counseling. But instead, he explained that he and his wife seek counseling for their relationship at designated checkpoints throughout the year to ensure they're on the same page.

This man was actually wonderfully happy in his marriage and counseling was a tool used to keep him that way.

He and his wife had adopted what I call a "maintenance mentality." This is just like when I fill my car with gas and take it in for oil changes. I don't wait until I run out of gas or until there is smoke billowing from the engine to start asking what went wrong. I value my car, so I complete regular maintenance to make sure it runs well.

Shouldn't we value the relationships in our lives more than a vehicle?

> *"We change our behavior when the pain of staying the same becomes greater than the pain of changing. Consequences give us the pain that motivates us to change."*
>
> **Henry Cloud**

Am I Prepared to Pay the Cost of Not Changing My Communication?

Every choice we make comes with a cost. Sometimes, there's a wonderful return on that investment, and sometimes we're left emotionally bankrupt.

When we begin to understand the potential cost of avoiding change, we can develop a clearer picture of what we're willing to let happen as a result of our inaction.

Some of our potential costs of not changing include:

- A messy and painful divorce
- Losing connection with the people in which you've invested so much time
- Lack of relationship with your children
- Shallow friendships that take more from you than they give
- A spiritual walk that is unfulfilling
- Feelings of regret for the things that you should have said or done

- Establishing unhealthy patterns of behavior for yourself and your children
- Going through life feeling utterly alone and unknown, even though you're surrounded with other people

These are just some of the costs we pay when we avoid making changes that can deepen our connections with others.

After knowing all that you could lose by avoiding these relationship and communication changes, there are some things to understand before implementing them in your life:

- These changes may be hard for you.
- It takes practice to get better at communicating.
- You'll need to ask for forgiveness at times.
- You'll need to ask for help, but you'll also learn how to do so.
- You're not alone in this process.

When you understand these things and commit to action, you'll realize that *no relationship is hopeless until you've decided that it is.* There is always room for hope and improvement.

The way you interact with people can always change for the better. Remember that your character and actions don't have to be dictated by the actions of others. Even if the other person in your relationship never changed one tiny bit for the better, your attitude and actions can change you.

Avoid getting stuck in the trap of waiting for others to change. You have to be willing to do the changing. You have to be willing to better yourself. Then, regardless of the outcome, you can know that you've done your best.

You might ask, "Do I always have to be the person to change or take initiative?" The simple answer is, "No. You don't." But when you get weary of taking the initiative and decide not to change, you leave the outcome up to others. You ensure that you're not being part of the solution, which in turn, makes you part of the problem.

Here's another way of looking at it. Which person in the relationship is responsible for initiating change? I would say that the one who feels they're more mature and reasonable should be the one to initiate change.

I'm guessing that most people in most relationships feel that they're the more rational and responsible party.

For example, in your relationships you most likely feel like you're the more developed person in terms of maturity and relational communication skills. I don't mean to burst your bubble, but if you're the one reading this, then you're the one that is responsible to change.

However, everything isn't your responsibility! Read on to discover some tools that will help you know exactly what is your responsibility moving forward and what isn't.

The Hold or Fold Principle

As a child learns to walk, it's important for parents to let them learn the concept of gravity. Learning to fall and stand up again is part of the development process. At this stage in a child's development, neurological pathways are forming that help the child and their decision making for the rest of their life.

Following a child around and controlling their every move may seem like a loving gesture to keep him from getting hurt. What is easy to forget is that we all have the potential to learn from our mistakes. When we're not allowed to fail, we lack the lesson or benefits of the experience.

Tim Sanford, a Focus on the Family Counselor, suggests a new way of thinking in relationships. He suggests that we can "Hold and Fold" or "Toss and Grab" in relational conflict.

The principle of Hold or Fold is something that was helpful to me when I was struggling to understand what role I play in my relationships. I was feeling overwhelmed and having trouble creating healthy boundaries. Others were manipulating me in asking me to take responsibility for things that were not mine to own. The problem was that as I was trying to be kind, I was letting people walk all over me.

This type of manipulative behavior has no place in healthy relationships. Often it's easy to place blame and consequences on others rather than deal with our own problems.

We also need to be able to distinguish between helping others and coming between them and natural consequences for their actions. Just as a child learns the natural consequences of gravity as they're learning to walk, we must let others learn certain things for themselves. This means that we stop taking responsibility for things that are not our doing.

Accepting responsibility for only what is yours to own is a significant component of creating healthy relationships. When we take responsibility for our part in relationships, and intentionally decide, "I'm an equal part in each of my relationships" we share equal accountability.

There are really four main actions that you can take in a relationship when you're having a conflict or deciding responsibility:

1. **Hold.** When you're able to hold what is truly yours, then you have taken full accountability for your actions, words, attitudes, judgments, past, and all the things that influence you.

   This is the part that you contribute to each of your relationships.

2. **Fold.** You fold when you're able to understand you have no accountability for the actions, words, attitudes,

judgments, past and everything else that influences the other person.

This is the part that the other person contributes, that you don't have control over.

3. **Toss.** This is where a person tries to throw responsibility that is theirs into the hands of another person.

   This action looks like blaming, making excuses, and limiting personal accountability.

4. **Grab.** This is where you try to take responsibility for actions or outcomes that are not yours to own.

   This action is an unhealthy pattern in relationships where you grasp for the blame, responsibility, or consequences when they should naturally fall on the other person.

The next time you're speaking to someone, observe and see which of these categories your communication is mimicking.

The healthiest relationships work from a "Hold and Fold" perspective.

Hold out your hands in front of you to help you better grasp this concept. Open your hands and know that the things you're responsible for fit in that limited space. When someone asks you to hold something that is their emotional responsibility, you can choose to fold your hands, almost like you're in prayer.

"Folding" is a respectful gesture. You're not pushing someone away, but simply avoiding accepting things that are not for you to hold. This also helps keep you from the temptation to grab at the problems of others or to push your problems on another person.

> *"Responsible is a compound word: response-able, meaning 'able to respond.' The only things you can legitimately respond to—the only things you can take 'ownership' of— are the things you have control over."*
>
> **Tim Sandford**, *Losing Control & Liking It: How to Set Your Teen (and Yourself) Free*

The Hold and Fold principle allows each person to be responsible for their own story. It lets people be responsible for their stake in the relationship. It also keeps us from trying to manipulate or change others and allows us to focus on growth within ourselves.

Assess which of these stages you communicate in most often. Then work to identify stages of others as you're speaking with them. Here are some examples to help you clarify the different stages.

This is a Toss/ Fold conversation:

> "Mom, I can't believe you won't give me the money to go out with my friends!"

> "Honey, you know where the chore list is located if you would like to earn some extra money for this weekend."

In this example the child is tossing blame at her mother while the mother holds her ground and reminds the child of a solution, without taking responsibility that is not hers.

This is a Hold/Grab conversation:

> "Mom, I know that if I had not procrastinated getting my chores done I could have chosen to go to bed much earlier yesterday."

> "Oh no, sweetheart! I should have known that you would be tired and done some of those chores for you or let you put them off a little longer."

In this example the child is taking responsibility for her actions and her lack of planning. The mother in this situation, however, is making excuses and trying to limit the consequences, instead of letting the child be responsible for her own choices.

Remember that staying within the Hold and Fold principle is the only way to ensure a balanced healthy relationship.

As important as it is to be a student of others, it's also equally important that you learn to be a student of yourself. Being a student of yourself means you learn that honesty is the best policy when it comes to self-evaluation.

In self-evaluation, it's imperative that you hold what is yours and fold the rest. It's so tempting to toss away responsibility or excuse your behavior. It's also tempting to take the blame for the actions of others. In an honest assessment of yourself, you must also have an honest analysis of what you find.

This is one of the first steps in having better communication: being honest about who you are and where you are in the scope of your life.

When you start to take full accountability only for what's yours, you start to have:

1. Less conflict in relationships
2. A clearer sense of self
3. A better ability to truly love others
4. More joy and peace

You'll have more of an understanding of who you are, why you're the way you are, and what you need when you're accountable only for what is yours.

When you gain this understanding, you're no longer a passive victim to your circumstances. You stop using phrases like "They made me so mad" or "That person always hurts my feelings." You take back control of what is yours and leave the rest.

You find yourself thinking healthy, affirming thoughts like:

- "I'm in control of myself."
- "I alone allow people to anger me."
- "I alone allow people to treat me poorly."
- "I alone can create new life in my relationships with my actions and attitudes."

Positive and Negative Costs

As we begin to evaluate ourselves, it's wise to count the costs of change, both positive and negative.

This can be a challenging exercise because people often aren't ready to take responsibility or accountability for what they *hold* in a relationship.

Let's take a moment to look at what could happen if you choose to implement these suggestions into your communication techniques. It's important you understand both the possible risks and gains of change.

The Risks

- It can cost you relationships when you elevate your level of communication. Sometimes, people are not ready to get to a place of accountability or honesty with themselves.

- These techniques could frighten the people in your life who are only looking for surface level connection with you. When you've been operating at low levels of connection and communication, you may find that some people aren't ready to deepen a relationship with you.

- People could begin questioning your motives as you try to change, especially in painful situations. If you're going through a painful separation or you have a broken relationship, others may want to know what your actual motivation is for "suddenly caring."

- You could be asked to deal with some painful feelings and uncomfortable self-disclosure as you go through this process.

- Looking at your past and then deciding about your future can be potentially painful. Many of us have some deep issues that need to be examined before we can move forward in our love for others.

- You may feel uncomfortable in disclosing part of your heart to those you want to be in a relationship with.

Possibly the hardest challenge of starting these techniques is deciding what you want to do with the information you've gathered. If the people around you are only operating in "Toss" or "Grab" thinking, there will likely be issues as you learn to take proper responsibility and leave the rest.

In taking inventory, you might see that there are relationships in your life that are better off severed: that they're toxic, unhealthy, or not serving either party's purposes anymore. People who tend to "Toss" have an especially hard time when someone decides to stop indulging their unhealthy behavior.

If you find that someone is unwilling to change their habits, it may be time to change the relationship. I will not pretend that this is easy. I want to warn you, as part of the process, there can be a loss of those toxic relationships. Even unhealthy relationships are ones in which you've invested time. If they need to be severed or changed, there is a grief process attached to this.

In counting the costs, remember that you'll likely fall back into old patterns of communication from time to time, forgetting the lessons and important skills that you've learned.

Another challenge you will face is failure to do everything perfectly. It is funny that we know this simple truth but are often surprised when we fail to perform at an optimum level. These failures and setbacks don't have to be a discouragement to you, but recognizing that they are coming is something that will assist you in this process.

Be patient with yourself and others, and remember that *lasting change takes time.* There is no "quick fix" when it comes to human behavior. This is a lifelong process of heart growth and change.

Last, you must face the fact that you could do everything right and the person you're trying to connect with could reject you or not get on board with having a deeper relationship with you. Again, there's a loss and a grief process that goes with that rejection.

As with any lasting changes, you can experience growing pains and strain those "emotional muscles" you haven't used in the past.

This is a process of development. You're going to be using communication skills, self-disclosure, and other skills that may be difficult to master.

Try to balance challenging yourself with cutting yourself some slack. Push your comfort zone while knowing your limits. Embrace these possible costs as the necessary investment for the projected returns in your relationships.

The Gains

Now that you've considered the costs, let's look at what you stand to win if you take the next step.

When you look at the positives, you realize you have the whole world to gain:

- Better relationships, with deeper connections
- Relationships that don't fall apart
- Relationships that know how to heal when there is hurt

- Greater contentment with your life and the people you're connecting with
- A total peace among conflict
- A life filled with much less drama
- A plan and new patterns of behavior that will serve you in every area of life

The work can be worth the cost when the end result is having deep, fulfilling, genuine relationships with those you love. Great relationships don't come about because of luck or circumstance, they happen because someone was willing to work without giving up.

> *"I'm a greater believer in luck, and I find the harder I work the more I have of it."*
>
> Thomas Jefferson

Who Do You Need Better Communication With?

Now that we have some general concepts down, let's get more specific and intentional about the relationships that need to change. There are a few ways you can go through this process of relationship renewal.

Depending on where you are in your life as you read this, you can choose how you would like to proceed. Choose what works best with your personality and current relational situations. Any of these techniques can be effective, so don't worry about choosing the wrong one. You can always change your mind and take a different approach.

Let's look at this process through the metaphor of a swimming pool. Everyone chooses to get into a swimming pool on a hot summer day in a unique manner. Instead of shoving you into this process, it is best if you choose your method of entry.

- You can jump into the deep end.
- You can wade into the shallow end.
- You can dip your toes in all over the pool to test the water.

Each of these techniques can help you move through the process. Here are some situations that might apply to each technique. You must choose what is right for you.

1. **Jump into the deep end.** Choose the most challenging relationship that you have right now. *This could be the first person you thought of when you picked up this book and hoped that things could change.*

   - With this method, you should be able to find out quickly if the person you want to connect with is going to cooperate with your proposed changes.

   - This method can be difficult if the relationship is already in crisis or in danger of becoming severed.

- In this method, you pick one relationship and focus your energy on applying as many of the concepts as possible.

2. **Wade into the shallow end.** Most people feel comfortable using this approach. Think of a few trusted people with whom you would like better connection and slowly try these principles while easing in at your own comfort level.

   - This method includes moving forward when things feel good, then pausing to get used to the water when things get uncomfortable. This is a great way to do things if you're committed to eventually being immersed in the water.

   - You're ready to "get wet," but you need time to process the information as you go.

   - This approach can be supplemented with the optional *30 Day Action Guide.* You can take one thought at a time and fully process it with manageable action steps and reflection.

3. **Dip your toes in all over the pool to test the water.** With this method, you might not have specific people in mind with which you need better connection. You plan to use these techniques to elevate connection with all the people in your life.

- Maybe you feel pretty balanced in your relationships so you don't want to be fully immersed, but you see the value of trying the concepts.

When you're able to identify which method you'll try first and have some specific relationships in mind, the principles in this book can be quickly applied in life and processed in your mind as you read.

I would encourage you to get as specific as possible about the people you wish to connect with. Generalizations are sometimes helpful, but they won't produce the deepest levels of growth and change. Name the person and relationships that you want to be intentional about changing.

As you read and learn these concepts, think of applying them in specific situations as much as possible.

Values and Main Statements

In order to enter into deeper relationships with others, we must better understand ourselves.

The objective is to get to a position where we know ourselves well enough to engage those around us at a meaningful level.

Before that point, relationships can feel like a façade, or fancy front. If you're not willing to be a student of yourself and participate in self-evaluation, how can you expect that someone else would open up to you?

We must be at a place where we're ready to examine our lives critically. This will ensure that at least one person in the relationship is working from a healthy self-awareness.

Values are the basis for how we live out our lives and how we process information and relationships. ***The values we hold outline how we interact and respond to the world and the people in it. Values are what we hold to be most important in our lives. When we're able to list the driving values in our life, we can understand the reasons behind what motivates us.***

For example, if the values in your life are being financially stable and having a beautiful home, then you know that your communication in your relationships will be driven with that desire in mind. This might look like a constant struggle with your spouse to spend less money. The fight is not primarily about the money, but the security and the home that the money represents.

If the value in your life is your family, again that will drive your actions, thoughts, attitudes, and types of relationships you choose to have. If family is your core value, then anything that compromises the family structure will be a non-negotiable issue for you. You'll set priorities that bring the value back to your family life and other things will become secondary.

When we stay true to our personal values and convictions, we find purpose for our lives. Then we can decide if our relationships are working for or against that purpose. Sometimes, the unease we feel in a relationship is a direct result of a clashing of values, not mere personality differences.

Defining the values and convictions that drive us is an important part of understanding who we are and is beneficial in elevating our relationships.

Listing those values can help you to connect and stay true to your own personal convictions and purposes. Think about the values and convictions that drive you. Take a moment and write down the top three values that you find are driving your life *right now.*

Values are a foundational principle in our lives, whether we recognize them or not. One of the biggest internal conflicts occurs when we have a value that is elevated in our minds but not in our actions.

This happens when we hold a particular value in high regard, but we don't live in accordance with the principles of that value. For example, you may say that you value financial security, but spend money frivolously when going out with friends. This is a misrepresentation of your values. Your thoughts and actions aren't connected.

When Actions Disconnect from Values, We Grow Apart

In my own life, there was once a time when my relationship with my husband was disconnected with my values. I especially valued having a deep relationship with him. I always knew this was a main value in my head and "on paper," but something wasn't right.

We would spend time together, but it wasn't fulfilling. We would eat together, but it didn't feel like we connected. We would talk, but it wasn't about anything substantial.

The relationship connection was happening, but at a surface level. My dissatisfaction with our connection level grew until I realized that I wasn't actually living my values with my actions.

My husband and I took inventory of why connection was becoming more and more difficult. We discovered that we were disconnected and distracted. Our connection was not being lost to lack of love, respect, or care for each other. It was being lost because of our priorities being given to other things that should have been secondary.

To counter this, we decided we needed to unplug from our phones, the TV, and the outside world while we ate together or had a conversation. Taking these easy steps allowed us to talk and share in more meaningful ways.

At first these interactions without distractions were a bit awkward because we had to focus to connect. Normally, we liked to relax by watching a show together or sitting next to each other while mindlessly playing with our phones. We thought these numbing activities were harmless and a way for us to relax. We were even counting that time as "quality time" together.

That could not have been farther from the truth.

It only took a few days of practice until we were both feeling more connected, fulfilled, and content with the time we were spending together. We had so much fun talking and laughing that neither of us even wanted to pick up our phones or turn on the television. We remembered that we were entertainment enough just with our own quirkiness.

Now we cherish our time to connect without distraction and we're remaining true to values we hold. This matching of values to actions is exactly what brings about a balance to life.

When our values were reflected in our actions, we were content. When our values were not being lived out, we felt disconnected.

It's important to get back to your core values and then implement those values in your life and relationships.

More Thoughts about Values

Here is one more vital note about values. When our values are ignored or not being fulfilled, we will have unrest in our lives and relationships. Values are tied to feelings of purpose and worth. They're not things to be taken lightly.

When you communicate with another person, listen for the things they value. These are the things that speak to their heart and define their character.

Even when there is conflict, look at values first and try for a solution second. When both people have their feelings and values heard, they're at a huge advantage for being able to work out a win-win solution that benefits the relationship as a whole.

> *"Try not to become a man of success.*
> *Rather become a man of value."*
>
> **Albert Einstein**

Chapter 6

Speak the Truth in Kindness

We're living in a world where people see truth as relative and extremely pliable. However, it's precisely this bending or manipulation of truth that can deteriorate the trust in a loving relationship.

Careful evaluation before speaking is one way to ensure you're speaking the truth in love and not saying something damaging for self-gain. There are numerous acronyms to help you pause and reflect before you speak. This is one that I have coined to help me in this process.

Before you speak, try asking yourself: "*Is this worth talking about?*"

Here are a few steps that can help you evaluate what you want to say, how you're going to say it, and what the outcome might be.

These steps can be expressed in the acronym TALK:

T: Truthful
A: Appropriate
L: Life-giving (or life-taking)
K: Kind

In the acronym TALK, we want to ask ourselves:

- **Is what I'm about to say truthful?** Is it truthful in the sense that it's completely true? Not a white lie, an exaggeration, or a minimizing statement?

- **Is this appropriate?** Is this an appropriate thing to say to another person? Is this an appropriate time to bring this information or comment to someone else's attention?

- **Is it life-giving or life-taking?** Is this something that will help the person or harm them? Am I speaking life into their situation or am I acting as a discouragement?

- **Are my words kind?** Are my words considerate, thoughtful, and encouraging?

Separately, each of these criteria could still cause some issues when you have a difficult conversation. But when you put these four ideas together, you can know that what you say is appropriate, thoughtful, and deliberate.

Depending on the situation, once you've gone through these four steps and determined if what you're about to say is truthful, appropriate, life-giving, and kind, then you can decide: ***Is this something that I actually need to say?***

Many times our conversations are unnecessary or contrary to our main goal of maintaining or growing strong relationships. They neither get our point across nor lift up the other person.

Asking yourself "Is what I have to say necessary?" helps you keep your personal opinions to yourself, while adding value to the conversation, as it's appropriate.

Just taking a moment to ask these simple questions can set you up to be a safe person for others. When someone knows that you think before you speak and what you say is meant for their good, they're more likely to listen and connect with you.

Consider these questions:

* Am I giving life to this person?
* Am I giving love?
* Am I giving excellent communication?
* Will this help the person and our relationship?

Let's phrase those questions differently:

* Am I taking life from this person?
* Am I giving impressions that are less than loving?
* Am I giving poor communication?
* Will this harm the person and our relationship?

This goes along with being kind, but it goes a step further. You can always be reflective of the purpose of your communication. You can ask "Is it in the best interests of the other person to hear this?" It's important to avoid speaking out of a selfish desire to be understood or heard. When you do this, you can lose sight of the person you're attempting to "help."

This method is a great way to be compassionate in your speech. Plus, you're better able to be heard and understood while maintaining the trust and rapport in a relationship.

If you use this TALK acronym in every relationship, you're bound to have less to be sorry for, fewer broken relationships, and fewer relational challenges.

Plus, when you go through the TALK questions before speaking, *you can extend a higher level of communication to all those you come into contact with.*

Balancing Truth and Kindness

There is an intricate balance between truth and kindness. These two concepts can almost seem to be opposites.

We have all heard the term "brutal honesty." However, honesty does not have to be brutal or harsh and it can still get the point across. A whispered truth is just as true as one that is shouted.

We must find a balance between the two ideals:

1. **Honesty.** We want people to be honest with us.

2. **Sensitivity.** We want people to take our feelings into account.

Remember, just because you speak something honestly doesn't mean you speak it in kindness. On the flip side, just because you're being kind doesn't mean you're being honest.

When you combine these into a balanced approach, not sacrificing either, then you discover a deeper level of communication.

You're not only honest and true to yourself, but also sensitive to both your needs and the needs of the other person. Reframe your thinking from a "brutal honesty" mentality to a mentality of "honesty with sensitivity." Being honest as well as a person of integrity is desired, but that integrity without tact is hardly ever received well. Speak the truth in love and watch how your relationship outcomes change for the better.

> *"Kind words can be short and easy to speak, but their echoes are truly endless."*
>
> **Mother Teresa**

Chapter 7

Have Values-Driven Conversations

I see a significant difference between people who speak from their values and those who don't.

When you speak from your values—from what's true to you—then you're speaking your most authentic truth. Whether or not the person agrees with you, they can connect with your passion and understand your values.

When you have a values-driven conversation, you value the other person's experience and values as well as your own. Also, you can connect deeper, avoid saying empty words, and spend time talking about the real heart of the issue.

Whenever you ask, "What does this person value?" you're able to deepen the conversation.

For example, if you're talking with someone and they're going on and on about their children and how much they love them, you can say, "This person probably values family. They probably value the love of their children and their home life."

When you listen to what people value, you can get to the heart of the matter.

Have you ever been in an argument that went something like this?

> Teenager: "Dad! It's not like I wrecked the car. I just got a speeding ticket."

> Dad: "It's not about the speeding ticket, but about your sense of responsibility for the safety of yourself and those around you."

Or maybe you can connect with something like this:

> Friend: "I'm sorry I was late."

> Other Friend: "It doesn't bother me that you were late as much as I wish you would have called to let me know so that I didn't worry."

There are surface level issues going on in these interactions, but there are also deeper values being expressed.

When we communicate, there is almost always something deeper fueling the conversation:

- When we're content, it's because things feel right with our hearts.

- When we're upset, it's because something doesn't sit well with our hearts.

- This is why we say "the heart of the matter." We understand that the heart is connected to the issue in ways that need to be recognized.

Try to look deeper than the initial "issue" and extract the values that are attached to the conversation. The disagreements you experience can be resolved much quicker if everyone involved recognizes the inherent values being expressed.

> *"The heart of the problem is a problem with the heart."*
>
> **Dr. Henry Brandt**

Chapter 8

Stay on Track with Your Conversations

To stay on track with your conversations, it helps to keep the purpose of the exchange in mind. Stop to assess if this is a light, transactional conversation. ***If you determine that it's a transactional exchange, then you know you don't want to make it a values-based conversation.***

Have you ever been talking to someone and asked yourself, "How did we get so off track?" This happens in relationships all the time. Transactional conversations can turn into deeper meaning conversations without you realizing it and usually one party leaves the other person behind.

Try to take a direct and intentional path in your conversations to avoid veering off onto hurtful side roads.

A great example of turning a transactional conversation into deeper issues would be an exchange between a teenager and her parents. Consider this common dialogue:

Mrs. Parentsknownothing: "How are you doing on your school project? Are you done or do you need some help?"

Miss Teen: "OH MY GOSH! I wish you would lay off of me! I'm not a child!"

Mrs. Parentsknownothing: "So . . . I will take that as a 'No, you don't need help'."

Miss Teen: "You always question what I'm doing instead of letting me be independent. My grades are fine but you never just trust me. All you do is nag!"

Mr. Parentsknownothing: "Miss Teen, answer your mother. Did you get that project done or not?"

Miss Teen: "You never listen to anything that I say. You don't care! I can't wait until I'm 18!"

Mrs. Parentsknownothing: (in a whisper) "Neither can I!"

You can see that the conversation started as a simple transactional question and it spiraled downward from there. The daughter obviously had some values issues waiting to explode and she assigned meaning to the conversation that was not originally there.

If both parties in the conversation knew how to stay on track with the conversation, the outcome might have been completely different. The daughter would know her parents were asking a transactional question that only needed a yes or no response. The parents would see there were deeper issues needing to be addressed concerning their daughter's feelings.

Many breakdowns in communication happen when we're starting in a transactional nature but then move unannounced into assigning meaning and value.

As a coach and counselor, I appreciate that it's useful for people to hear back what they've said. It helps me, as the listener, to ensure I hear them fully. My reflection of their words allows them to look back on what they've said and determine if it matches their own needs. It also allows them to hear their own voice.

It can also provide an opportunity for someone to make a correction, address an assumption, or catch incorrect wording.

For example, if a client is speaking and I speak back their words or a summary of their thoughts, they can say, "Well that's not really what I meant," or, "Wow, I guess I've never said that out loud before."

Remember that words are powerful. We should reflect at certain points in the conversation, reiterate what somebody said, or ask for meaning behind what was said. Oftentimes, *it can open the eyes of both the speaker and the listener.* Both parties can then recognize the greater meaning of their words.

Let's look back on the exchange between the teenager and her parents. There are some important lessons from this exchange that we can learn. If either the daughter or the parents chose to break the cycle of poor communication, the outcome could have been positive.

It only takes one person to change the nature of communication. It takes one person reflecting or clarifying to change how an interaction is being perceived. There is power in knowing that individual action can shape group dynamics!

Remember that even if the other person in the communication remains volatile, you still have a choice about how you react. Ask yourself, "Am I adding value to this conversation or just fuel for the fire?" When you've honestly made this assessment, you can go back to the principle of "Hold or Fold" and move forward with confidence.

Stay on track with the topic of conversation and move forward to finding understanding with others. If the conversation starts to get off track, be the first to recognize this and steer it back in a healthy direction.

Think for a moment about the grooves and bumps on the edge of a highway. They're there to alert the driver they're about to veer off the road. The driver then knows that they need to make a correction in their course.

Often we see that we're veering off the conversation, but we don't stop it from becoming a destructive mess. As the driver of the conversation, are you content to let things spiral out of control, or are you willing to make a correction that could save everyone lots of hurt and potential damage?

Watch for the warning signs that the conversation is heading in a destructive direction and make corrections before it's too late.

> *"Stay focused instead of getting offended or off track by others."*
>
> **John C. Maxwell**

Chapter 9

When to Utilize Emotion and When to Dump it at the Door

A skilled communicator is always able to assess when it's appropriate to express certain emotions and they know when those emotions cloud the purpose of the conversation.

All relationships have reoccurring conflicts. Those redundant conflicts can bring us to a place of frustration where we forget to use communication skills and slide back into unhealthy patterns instead.

Let's explore a common conflict that happens in homes everywhere. For most couples and families, the issue of household chores seems to be one of those redundant topics that rears its ugly head at the most inopportune times.

For example, in my home, my husband and I have each agreed to complete certain household tasks. One of the jobs that my husband has on his list is putting away the clean laundry.

Here are two examples of ways we could deal with the issue of my husband not getting this task accomplished. **I will show you *how to go from a transactional communication to an emotional communication* and what the difference is between the two.**

In a transactional conversation, I would ask my husband, "Did you do the laundry?" or, "Will you get the laundry put away?" It's a straightforward, yes or no question. There isn't emotion loaded into it. In this case I need to watch my tone, inflection and body language to make sure I am not communicating underlying issues with my actions. A transaction is not loaded with emotion or meaning. The purpose of a transaction is to give or gain information.

When I come into the room and I have emotion loaded into the question, I could start the conversation by saying, "Why is the laundry never done?" or "You don't appreciate what I do. You can't even do your one job."

You can see the difference between making a simple statement or asking a basic yes or no question and coming in with emotions, values, and feelings flooding the conversation.

We're no longer talking about laundry in the emotional example. We're talking about my feelings.

Emotional intelligence is a key indicator of relationship success. It is crucial that I understand my emotions but it is equally important that I control when and how I express them. Emotions can get in the way of direct communication. I'm not stating that emotions have no place in communication, but it's in direct communication at a transactional level that emotional speaking hinders the process of communication instead of enhancing it.

When you use extreme words like "always" and "never," those messages simply are not true. ***It's important to avoid using these extremes because they don't accurately describe the message you're trying to convey.*** Even with practice, this principle is difficult to implement.

Now when either my husband or I use the words "always" or "never," we use humor to remind the other person how ridiculous those statements sound. He might squeak in an obnoxious voice "always never," and it instantly gets my attention. I usually laugh and rephrase what I was saying to be more accurate. Speaking in extremes is a hard habit to break!

Using these extreme words demonstrates an inaccurate perspective. The truth is there have been times when my husband has done the laundry. He's not *always* forgetful. So when I use those words, "always" and "never," I'm showing that my perspective is tainted.

Before you enter into a conversation that you know you may have trouble with emotionally, unload your verbal machine gun. Don't come in shooting and expect anything but a mess to result.

Begin by gathering information and then make some deliberate choices about what action needs to be taken. Choose your questions based on the desired result of the communication. ***Do you need information or do you need a conversation?*** These are two different needs that require two different approaches.

Try to be as objective and truthful as possible in your relationships. This can save so much relational heartache. Seek the truth and live in reality with the people that you love. Reality is not always as kind as our perception of how things are, but it's the only foundation that can create lasting change.

> "*If you want to feel deeply, you have to think deeply. Too often we separate the two. We assume that if we want to feel deeply, then we need to sit around and, well, feel. But emotion built on emotion is empty. True emotion—emotion that is reliable and does not lead us astray— is always a response to reality, to truth.*"
>
> **Joshua Harris**

Chapter 10

Expressing Your Emotions Effectively

Now that we've talked about how to leave emotion out of a conversation when needed, we can move to learning how to use emotion in conversation effectively.

Honesty is valuable and needs to be a priority in your relationships. When you have emotions, you should be honest about them.

However, getting emotional is very different than expressing what emotion you're feeling. Expressing emotion is telling someone how you feel and why. Getting emotional is usually expressed when you act out of control.

We don't want to use our emotions as a weapon, but rather as a tool.

As emotions come up, we want to be able to express them honestly, but with a level of self-control. If you need to cry, you want it to be because you're passionate or sad and that crying is a natural expression of your feelings. You don't want to use your emotion to manipulate the other person.

When you're angry, it's okay to express the fact that you're angry or frustrated, but yelling is an example of *getting emotional* instead of *expressing your emotion*.

It's okay to state honestly how you're feeling, but when we get emotional and our tone raises, our volume increases, or our actions start to become out of control, we lose credibility with the other person in the conversation.

We want to make sure we're expressing how we feel, without being overly emotional.

As usual, I'm going to suggest the common sense approach of maintaining a balance. **Honesty with your emotions is central to your well-being.** You need to be honest about what you feel, but again, you don't necessarily have to show the full expression of your emotions.

You can say emphatically, but calmly, "I'm frustrated," "I'm scared," or, "I don't like what's happening right now." You can do that without being out of control of your emotions.

We want to ensure our honesty doesn't hurt someone else, even if it's a statement of fact. I've found that, in the name of emotional honesty, I was often being quite cruel to the people who upset me. I would justify my words of critique by saying "statement of fact" before I dug into what a person said or did that bothered me.

I made this statement to ease my own conscience about being negative about another person's actions or behavior.

This was really a cover up for me being out of control. I realized that I was responsible for my feelings and actions, and that even though I may be able to say, "FACT! That guy is rude," it was not the best approach for solving problems or restoring relationships.

If the tables were turned, I could have easily reflected some "facts" back on myself. "FACT! I am being overly sensitive and gossipy" or "FACT! I need an attitude adjustment."

When it comes to other people, I can quickly point out shortcomings and areas of improvement. That energy would be better spent in self-evaluation and growth. In learning this I realized that I can close my eyes to the ugly attitudes I see in myself or I can keep my eyes open and adjust the picture

We need to be careful with our emotions. The fact that you feel a certain way doesn't give you the right or permission to act that feeling out to the detriment of another person.

You can often see this behavior in children because of their lack of self-control. They have not yet learned that their feelings, although valid, don't give them permission to move into destructive action.

Consider this example:

Mom: "Why did you hit your sister and pull her hair?"

Child: "She would not share her toys and she made me mad!"

The mother knows that her child's interaction was not healthy. In the mind of the child, however, his actions may have been perfectly justifiable. In his mind, his lashing out was merely "cause and effect."

Many people take this attitude into adulthood, and it makes for caustic relationships down the road. Imagine if the child's view of his actions was never challenged or corrected. He could easily escalate his behavior as life and circumstances continued to anger and frustrate him.

Let's take a look at this child as a grown up:

Police: "Why did you hit your girlfriend?"

Man: "She disrespected me and pushed my buttons. She knows exactly what to say to send me over the edge!"

It's clear there is a lack of personal responsibility being taken. Before the child is an adult, and in better control of his actions, we might intervene with discipline to teach the child that his actions are not appropriate. To the child, it might seem like a life sentence as he is sent to time out, but it's nothing compared to the consequence he could have later in life if he maintains the same unhealthy logic.

I am not suggesting that children who hit their siblings will one day become violent offenders, but you can see that, when wrong thinking is left unchallenged, wrong assumptions can carry over into adulthood.

This example of lashing out crossed the line into the physical realm, but *it's no better when we lash out and "hit" people with our words.* Often we excuse emotional and psychological abuse in our relationships because our definition of abusive behaviors stops at causing physical harm. Abuse comes in many forms and has no place in relationships defined by trust and genuine love.

Putting this into practice means customizing your responses to how the other person might interpret your words. This means taking full control of your actions instead of letting them be guided solely by your emotions.

Coming to a conversation with a balanced approach can mean more peaceful outcomes and better communication in the future.

You may be thinking "Okay, I can try that, but what if things get out of control?" When the situation has already escalated beyond the point of no return, becoming more emotional is definitely unwise, although it will feel like a natural response. Don't blindly follow what "feels natural" without applying wisdom to the situation.

For example, if I were stranded at sea, it would feel natural for me to drink the water around me. We all know that this would have dire consequences even though my mind would have assured me this was a helpful way to alleviate my thirst. Often your mind will assure you that anger, lashing out and abuse tactics will help you get your way when in reality they allow in something poisonous to the relationships you are trying to save.

When feelings have already been hurt, you want to de-escalate the conversation, not add more fuel to the fire.

Sometimes the safest bet is to ask for a pause in the conversation so that emotions have some time to cool down. This can help you avoid saying things you may regret and keep your conversation productive. Express your emotions in a manner that brings life to your connections. Resist the urge to "drink in" what is around you and what feels natural. Instead, opt for wisdom that can help rescue your relationships.

> *"I don't want to be at the mercy of my emotions. I want to use them, to enjoy them, and to dominate them."*
>
> **Oscar Wilde**, *The Picture of Dorian Gray*

Chapter 11

Change Your Method of Questioning to Get Better Answers

I t has been said that we're human *"beings"* not human *"doings."* This means that asking people how they're doing isn't always the best or most productive of questions.

When you ask people how they're functioning in life, at a passionate level, you get a glimpse of their heart and it can't help but connect you.

You want to elevate the conversation, but it may seem awkward to ask "How are you being?" When you're curious about learning about another person, it's crucial that you find ways to elevate your questioning. This might look like asking, "What is changing you right now?" or "What in your life are you proud of that you could share with me?"

These questions help you raise the bar on communication. It also means you're creating space for the other person to share deeper ideas.

You don't have to actually ask someone "how are you being" to get specific about what you would like to know. Ask about information and experiences that will connect you with the person you're talking with.

Some intentional questions you might ask are:

- What are you learning in your life right now?
- What is the greatest barrier/struggle for you right now?
- Are you feeling content with your life? Why or Why not?
- How are you working to overcome the obstacles in your way right now?
- How can I support you?
- How can I partner with you?
- Tell me about something that you're really excited about right now.

Asking these kinds of questions assesses how the person is "being" versus just getting a surface level answer of, "I'm fine" or "I'm good." Intentional questions dive into the deeper meaning of what's going on in their life, which is what you want to know. You're striving to make connection meaningful, and specific questions like these help you to do that.

These questions can be used universally, but they're more natural in established relationships. You usually won't ask a stranger these questions or delve into them in a transactional conversation.

Save these questions for when you have time to be with someone and intentionally listen to their response. Don't attempt these questions in a "drive by" manner and expect a healthy result. Learn to only ask a question when you're willing to take the time to invest in the answer.

When I start a conversation asking something more intentional, I'm deliberately establishing the direction of the whole conversation to create a more profound connection for both of us.

I have come to see that elevating my questions has had a profound impact on my connection with others. Justin and Trisha Davis, authors of *Beyond Ordinary*, have some great examples of questions that can change a marriage.

In an effort to deepen my marriage, I used some of their questions and techniques. I learned to ask my husband deeper questions which in turn gave us a deeper connection. This has been a catalyst in changing the depth of our communication. Some of the more intentional questions I ask now on a regular basis are:

- **How can I support and pray for you?** This helps him to know I'm in support of him and I want to understand the things that worry him. I'm fully participating as his partner when I know what things are on his heart.

- **How can I be more intimate with you?** This helps him to see I care about our connection, both physical and emotional. This also helps to reveal areas of neglect in our relationship.

- **How can I love you better?** This helps him to know that I love him with intention. Notice that I don't ask how I can love him "more." I love him plenty, but when I ask about loving him better I'm able to hear specifically what he needs from me to feel connected.

Asking these questions connected us powerfully. This got us talking and the answers that came from our questions were actually helpful. The results are so much better using this method than when I used to ask, "How can we make our relationship more fulfilling?" This question was not good at addressing what I wanted to know. It was also too broad for me to understand specifics of what would be helpful for relational growth.

These questions can be powerful in all of your relationships, not just in marriage. Many times in close relationships we try to get this result with broad and unspecific questions, such as:

- "What do you want from me?"
- "Why can we never seem to get on the same page?"
- "What's the matter?"

In these examples, we're asking the wrong questions. When asked to answer these questions, we can feel overwhelmed, trapped and lost.

Action Tip

Find a time to write down what you would like to know from another person and then formulate open-ended questions to help facilitate that conversation. Determine a time that is appropriate to have this more intimate and vulnerable conversation.

Finding a Good Time for Your Intentional Questions

In deeper questioning, as with everything else, timing is key.

If somebody is feeling extremely emotional or distressed, it's not the time to ask them one of these deeper questions, because they may not be ready to engage.

This is the same kind of situation as when someone is noticeably upset and you ask them, "How are you doing?" or, "What's wrong?" and they respond with, "Fine" or, "Nothing."

If that's their response, they're not willing to go to a deeper place of connection at that time. They need to be left alone to pause and process whatever it is that's going on within them. Try to discern if you should push ahead with questioning or if you need to give them some time to process.

This can actually be a huge gift to the person that you care about. Giving them time to process means you give them permission to sit with their emotions and formulate their reactions. Take the pressure off yourself and realize you don't need to "fix" anything.

Being able to discern good timing is vital to good relationships. Remember also that *your* timing is not always the timing that is the best. People who have mastered this are able to step into the shoes of those around them. They assess the situation and all of the factors with wisdom. Then they decide if the timing allows for finding a positive solution.

There is no such thing as perfect timing when we try to initiate difficult conversations or complex connections. ***There is, however, bad timing and better timing that can make or break the outcome.***

Elevate and open your questioning. Your questions, when well thought out, can bring you answers and truth that you never knew existed. The way you choose to question is the way others usually choose to respond. When you elevate the question, you elevate the conversation, the answer, and the relationship!

---

*"Judge a man by his questions
rather than by his answers."*

Voltaire

Chapter 12

Listen for Meaning, Not Just Content

Most of us grew up knowing that any good story was made up of the five "W's": Who, What, When, Where and Why. These guidelines gave us an outline of what the story contained and the message that we could glean from the story itself. The same principle can be applied to the "story" of your conversations and relationships.

Take a moment to evaluate the reason that you listen to others. Are you listening to appease, rebut, or argue your point? The motivation behind your listening cannot be anything but hearing and understanding if you expect relational growth to happen.

Someone shared with me recently that he tends to listen to "appease" others in order to avoid conflict. He didn't realize that by doing this he was actually creating more conflict. In listening to "appease," he was shutting down the conversation and not being true to his real opinions.

Now, instead of listening to avoid conflict, he is committed to listening as an active participant in the communication. This small change is going to make a huge impact on his life and relationships.

Begin to listen in your relationships for the meaning behind the words people say. This is not about making assumptions, but about looking for what is actually being communicated. You've elevated some of your questioning and now it's time to elevate your listening.

When you're listening for meaning, first listen for the *"who"*:

* Who are they talking about?
* Who is the subject of the conversation?
* What is their connection to this person?
* What is their tone about this person?

When you focus on questions like these, you can understand who the person is talking about and get some background on them (if they're frustrated with them, if they're excited about them, etc.) and hear some of the feelings that are associated with that person.

Next, listen for the *"what"*:

* What are they saying is the issue?
* Are they bringing up deeper issues?
* What values are being attached?
* What are they asking for?
* What do they need?
* What is troubling them?

When you begin to listen for meaning and not just content, these are the things to ask yourself as you engage with others.

Lastly, ask the "*why*":
* Why are they feeling this way?
* Why are they choosing to communicate this way?
* Why is it important for them to express this thought to me at this time?
* Why is their reaction so strong right now?

By assessing the *who,* the *what,* and the *why* of the conversation, you're digging into the meaning the person is trying to convey, not just the story or content.

The *when* and the *where* questions are addressed more as we look at good timing and position for having meaningful conversations.

When you listen for meaning and not just content, you're intentionally listening on a deeper level. The person may not actually be saying anything more profound, but you're hearing more profoundly what they're trying to convey.

This is critical because, as you reflect back to them what you heard, you can feel a deeper connection. You can hear the heart of the matter. You can hear what they are passionate, sad or scared about.

When you listen with intention, you can hear the person's heart, not just their words.

The main obstacle with listening for meaning is that you bring your own perspectives and assumptions. This can be dangerous. You don't want to assume what someone else is feeling or meaning. Assuming and wondering are two different things. Keep a mind of wonder and not of assumption as you listen.

To reflect back to them, ask, "Is this what you meant?" or, "I heard this from you. Is that accurate?" so you're not making any incorrect assumptions. Instead, you're connecting with them in a way that builds understanding and a stronger relationship.

It's crucial to listen for what people are asking you to hear and not just what you think they mean.

> *"Most people don't listen with the intent to understand; they listen with the intent to reply."*
>
> **Stephen R. Covey**, *The 7 Habits of Highly Effective People: Powerful Lessons in Personal Change*

Chapter 13

Speak with Meaning, Not Just Content

I t has always been important to me to be a person of integrity. To me, this has meant that I say what I mean and I mean what I say. In order to do this effectively, I needed to learn the skill of speaking from a place of intention.

This is where we move from transactional conversation to deeper connection.

One of the things you want to do as you move from transactional conversation to deeper connection is ***inject action and emotion words into the conversation.*** Try to connect to your emotions and the actions those emotions influence.

One of the key signs that you're moving from finding information into that deeper conversation is that you're including action words and descriptions of your emotions. As you function with other adults, you can ask for action or talk about your feelings and reactions in ways that encourage the other person to engage in a meaningful exchange with you.

Also, you're assessing the meaning of your words and tone. Your tone and intention has the potential to change the whole demeanor of another person for the good of the relationship or for the destruction of the relationship.

It's easy to make this harder than it needs to be. Think of someone interacting with an infant. Most people unconsciously try to speak words and use gestures to make the baby smile or react. You know it doesn't matter much what you say to a baby, as long as your tone is in tune with making the baby happy.

Also, this exchange usually has an "other's-focused" agenda. Think about the deeper implications of that. You may be having the worst day ever, but if you're holding a baby and making him laugh, I hardly can imagine you would be able to sit there stone faced. Laughing is contagious and you would smile and laugh as well, although the baby is not engaging in the interaction for *your* amusement.

This is an example of pure, other's-focused interaction. In the end, smiles are exchanged and we understand that, regardless of what was said, feelings and actions were displayed that provided a connection.

Contrary to what this world may tell you to believe, it is this focus on others that can bring us the greatest joy. This is another truth to balance in your pursuit of better relationships. You must focus on yourself to grow, but you must focus on others to truly change.

When you move from transactional to deeper connection, *you begin with the end in mind. You understand that the end goal is to connect,* to understand and to be understood.

In a transactional conversation, the end goal is to get a yes or no answer or to glean information. That's the main difference. *In a conversation where you're moving to connection, you're striving to unite with another person, not just learn facts.*

Deeper connection in relationships is usually going to be with a spouse, friend or child. These are the people that you want to be in your life for the long term, that you value and want to better understand.

Life is all about finding meaning. You find meaning when you look for it. In the world and in relationships, where you cannot find significance, you feel utterly alone. Make sure to add meaning and intention into your conversations. Again, it starts with the end in mind.

What is your goal?

* I want to make someone laugh.
* I want to get some information.
* I want to connect and make this person feel heard.
* I want this person to walk away knowing they're loved.

This intentional assigning of meaning is powerful. It means that, regardless of the content of your conversation, there is value to the connection because of how you speak, listen and respond.

Your values should flow from you because they're a deeply imbedded part of you. Seek to be a person of integrity that has a life overflowing with meaning and purpose. Remember, it's far more powerful to *show* people meaning through your life than to try and convince them with your words.

"Don't explain your philosophy. Embody it."

Epictetus

Chapter 14

Naturally Bring the Conversation Back to Values and Meaning

L ike most people, I tend to look for the path of least resistance. I want to naturally connect better with others without trying to reinvent the foundational concepts of human interaction. The most effective way to naturally connect in a conversation is to relate back to what each person values.

As you look at speaking and listening for deeper meaning, an important concept to understand is that it's okay to ask questions. ***It's okay to ask the person if there's a deeper meaning or emotion they're trying to convey.***

If you're sensing there may be a deeper meaning, instead of just assuming, take a moment and ask the person to clarify for you what they're feeling or what they might be trying to say to you. Attempt to identify and clarify the values that the person is expressing.

It's fine to ask if part of the conversation angers or saddens the other person. When you have this insight, you can work on listening more or finding a solution to the problem, whichever is more appropriate.

Before you dive into this, though, you might want to go back to determining the answer to the question "Is this transactional or is this conversation for connection?"

Next, look for what values are being supported or ignored. As you're trying to connect with someone and you're assessing what values are being talked about, you can start to assess, *"Is the person supporting the values they're sharing or are they ignoring those values?"*

You can also do a self-check at this point to see if the person is speaking to values you hold dear or values you find unimportant.

Last, ask, *"What can I do differently?"* This is an action-oriented question. You can bring the conversation to a different level by asking what actions you can take that would make the situation better.

In this way, you're taking responsibility in your relationship while at the same time acknowledging there are things that could change.

Here is the process broken down:

1. Listen for meaning.
2. Listen for values.
3. Listen for what you're responsible for.

Interrupt the cycle and insert new action for a different result.

In talking with the mother of a dear friend, I saw this point illustrated so potently. For years, she had felt unloved by her in-laws. She was constantly criticized by her husband's family and she felt unwelcome. She dreaded spending time with that side of the family, knowing the outcome would be feeling hurt and then the resulting conversation would ensue where her husband explained away the behavior of his family or simply did not hear or see it happen.

The husband grew up in this dysfunction and so the unhealthy behavior was something he had learned to tune out.

Now wouldn't it be wonderful if I could tell you the story ended when all of the husband's family realized their destructive behavior and transformed into loving, uncritical people? They embraced their daughter-in-law and they all lived happily ever after. News flash! Sometimes you can't fix crazy. To this day, the family still wallows in their dysfunction, but the young couple did something that changed the cycle!

In a counseling session, the wife was reiterating her hurt feelings about the husband's lack of understanding and support. The counselor gave the husband a challenge. The next time they went to his family's house, he was to pay attention only to his wife. He was to listen to her words and see the feedback she got. He was to focus on her and see things from her perspective.

After an evening with his family, the couple got in the car to drive home and the husband exclaimed, "My family is crazy. Every time you said something, even in agreement, they turned it into an argument."

The wife finally felt the justification she needed. She finally felt heard and understood. They spoke about the behavior and the fact that the husband was unable to see it in the past. This one interaction changed everything. In re-telling this story to me, the wife said something so profound: "I never needed the approval of his family. What I needed was to know that my husband was behind me no matter what."

Do you see how the issue was not about the issue? After this experience, the wife was able to let the petty comments of the family roll off without upsetting her. The real problem was she wanted her husband to see her pain and understand her.

We can all take a lesson from this story. Sometimes the problem doesn't have to be "solved" in the traditional sense. People need to know their feelings and values are being heard and understood. Many times, feeling understood can replace the need for a solution especially when the solution involves waiting for the actions of others to change.

Have you ever had the same conversation with someone over and over? Can I get an AMEN! This happens to all of us and we seem to lack the tools for changing the conversation and getting unstuck.

When the same fight or point has been brought up again and again, it's because in at least one person's mind, the issue has not been resolved. That's the best time to move into deeper meaning and take the conversation back to values.

When you move into feelings, values, and meaning, you realize why the issue continues to be re-hashed.

Interrupt the cycle and ask, "What is underneath this issue?" If the problem is recurring, then you can be certain that one or both parties are not having their values and feelings validated. The "issue" is not only about the "issue." We have these cyclical conversations because we haven't gone through the work of understanding and empathizing with one another completely.

Stopping the cycle doesn't mean we agree or that we even have a solution. It means we've worked through the issue with the intention of *understanding* and *honoring* the feelings and fears of the other person.

It's critical to stop sidestepping the real problems and start to face them head on. Going around and around isn't working. By trying to avoid the harder work, you're creating a much bigger problem. Be the person to throw a stick in the wheel and interrupt the cycle of negative communication.

When you bring the conversation back to basic feelings and values, you have the power to make someone feel heard, loved, and understood.

People that are heard, loved, and understood don't need to fight and prove a point. They don't need to win. And they don't need to re-hash. *This is the real solution to so many of your relational problems.*

It's not about winning, compromise, or finding the answer to a problem. It comes down to people feeling like they're able to trust in their relational connections as a safe place to be heard and understood. If you keep trying to go around this process, you'll keep having the same results. To move past the issue, you must first get to the heart of it.

"The best way out is always through."

Robert Frost

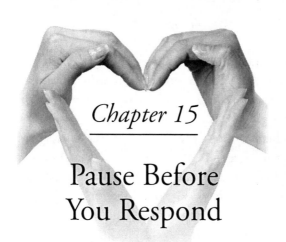

Chapter 15

Pause Before You Respond

When you stop and let your mind process your surroundings, you can fully experience the moment. This is the same concept as "stopping to smell the roses." It means you're taking the time to notice what is important and beautiful about life.

Likewise, when you pause and take a moment to process what the other person is saying before you respond to them, it lets them know they're valuable and worth listening to.

Pausing allows you to collect your thoughts. Each day, you're processing millions of pieces of information all at the same time. When you purposely quiet the brain, you let people know they're worth stopping for. You also give yourself the opportunity to think before you speak.

Think of how much conflict could be avoided if we all had a ten second buffer in our brains before words were allowed to come out! What if a pop up window appeared that said "Are you sure you want to send this message?"

You add value to the conversation by internally thinking before you externally speak.

When you take the time to pause, you're giving yourself permission to reset the conversation. Once you pause, you can continue in the direction a conversation is going or you can choose to change the direction.

When you're overwhelmed, emotionally out of control, or frustrated, this pause technique is great for helping you navigate to a better end result. Give yourself permission to stop and ask, "Do I continue down this path or do I choose another?"

Pausing like this lets you take responsibility for the choices you make instead of living life on auto-pilot.

Especially when you're frustrated or overwhelmed, this is a helpful technique to make some choices and be intentional about how the conversation is going to end. Go back to the principle of beginning with the end in mind.

There are pros and cons to this "living in the moment" mentality many of us have tried to adopt. Being present is important, but allowing the moment to carry you away without weighing the consequences is simply not wise. When you're totally living in the moment, you're more likely to say things you don't mean. You make declarations and promises you cannot keep because consequences outside that moment are not being weighed.

Mastering this process is like making the transition from adolescence to adulthood. It can be painful and not so pretty, but it's worth it.

A main reason that adolescents are able to "live in the moment" comes down to brain function and development. They're physically not as capable as adults when it comes to predicting future outcomes and consequences. The part of their brain that processes information, consequences and impulse control isn't developed fully.

As an adult, you have much more responsibility to others, and your brain not being developed is usually not an excuse that is going to fly with your loved ones. Notice that I said that you're more responsible *to* others, but not *for* others.

You must choose for your language and thinking to pass the junior high level. Graduate yourself into the idea that your actions and words carry consequences that need to be carefully understood and thought out.

When you don't pause, there is collateral damage. When you think about where a conversation went wrong, you'll almost always realize it was something you didn't mean or you went off on a track that wasn't relevant or kind.

Looking back on a conversational disaster, most people can say, "I just didn't think about it," or, "I didn't mean to say that," or, "That's not what I intended."

These situations arise when you don't take the time to pause. Usually you refuse to stop and think because you feel it takes too much time or effort. The opposite is actually true. You can pause now and use caution or you can stop everything later to clean up your mess. Which would you prefer?

Here is an acronym to help you remember to PAUSE:

P: Participate fully in the connection
A: Account for your reaction and response
U: Utilize what you know to be true
S: Suspend judgment
E: Enter back into the connection with confidence

Let's take a look at what each of these steps can tell us:

1. **Participate fully in the connection.** Eliminate distractions and focus on the person you're talking with and the values they bring to the conversation.

2. **Account for your reactions and responses.** Consider how your reactions and responses may be taken, as well as whether or not they're helpful. Think about the end result that you hope to see.

3. **Utilize what you know to be true.** Try to find truth in what the other person said before you respond. Then understand how your view of truth is the same or different.

4. **Suspend judgment.** Look at the other person's perspective and try to refrain from implementing judgment.

Instead of judgment, exercise discernment. Try to discern what the best course of action might be and how your relationship might be affected.

5. **Enter back into the conversation with confidence.** Ensure you fully understand what's going on, that you're accountable for your reactions, that you've looked at the facts as well as your emotions, and that you have control over how you want to express your thoughts.

When you allow yourself to become upset, angry, or confused, it's difficult to participate fully in the connection.

When you stop and put yourself to the side for a moment, it gives you a chance to understand things from another perspective. *Then, you're able to come back into the conversation in a way that's productive, not just emotion-driven.*

Also, this pause isn't for trying to figure out what the other person might be trying to convey. This pause is really for getting yourself under control. When you've taken some time to pause, you'll notice that your conversations in general are elevated—that you stop rashly and heatedly coming in and out of conversations.

Those around you will also feel heard and will be more willing to have conversations with you because it's a more pleasant experience.

The best part of this technique is the satisfaction of knowing you came in and out of the conversation with the highest integrity. You used discernment and not harsh judgment, and you began with the integrity of the relationship in mind.

This PAUSE process takes no more than 10 or 15 seconds and can bring you closer connections with those you love.

It also reminds you that you're in control of yourself and how you choose to respond. It only takes one person who is willing to break the cycle for major change to happen!

Consider the cost of responding without taking pause. It may not always end in disaster, but it also may not be the most elevated form of communication you could muster. There can be power in silence and reflection that far outweighs words spoken in haste.

> *"The right word may be effective, but no word was ever as effective as a rightly timed pause."*
>
> **Mark Twain**

at you appreciate and love about them and watch th
ngs happen:

1. They will cherish the affirmation.
2. It reinforces the behavior and makes them want to continue doing it.

We're blessed to be able to tell people that we love hem. We can increase the blessing by telling them why.

> *"It should be a privilege to be able to say 'I love you' to someone. It shouldn't be something people say just because they feel like it. A privilege that is earned. They say you have to earn the right to be loved; no, love is unconditional, if you love someone, they don't have to earn it. But the right to tell someone that you love them? That has to be earned. You have to earn the right to be believed."*
>
> **C. JoyBell C.**

Chapter 16

Elevate the Conversation and Your Connection

Do you ever feel completely misunderstood by the people in your life? Chances are those same people have felt the same way. We all have a tendency to feel like an issue is ours alone to bear and we forget that others struggle with the same feelings and pain that we do.

When we turn the focus from ourselves to others, we can learn how to elevate our conversations and connections.

However, if you truly don't *know* another person, elevation of the conversation is difficult. **Be a student of those around you.** Look for the things that excite people. Pay attention when you see that someone is scared or hurt. This study of others pays off and will allow you to connect in an elevated manner.

139

When you discover the love and fear triggers of the people you're close to, you can speak to them at an elevated level.

For example, early in my marriage, I realized I wanted to be intentional with my words because of the impact that they have on my husband.

I became a student of my husband and realized that he needed to know specifically what I loved about him. He needed respect and feedback that let him know I appreciate and honor him as a person. I decided to limit the number of times in a day I simply said, "I love you," to my husband. I did this not to withhold loving words from him, but to become more intentional about what I specifically meant by "I love you."

People need to hear "I love you," and we should say it regularly, but more importantly we need to find ways to show it as well. "I love you" is wonderful to hear, but for some reason, after a time, the impact of those words can wear off and seem less meaningful.

Part of this may be an issue with the English language. Think about the implications of having such a huge, complex feeling like love wrapped up into only one word.

* I love my iced caramel macchiato on a hot day.
* I love those shoes I saw at the store.
* I love that new song on the radio.
* I love the feeling of a job well done.
* I love my husband.

All of these statements begin with the sam   w
that doesn't mean they're equal to me in value.   th
I might express more love for my iced carame
than my husband, but they're not even on the sa
level . . . usually.

I learned to change my "I love you" into
more specific—something that conveyed what I
the same time spoke to what he needed to hear.

One of the statements I've used to replace, "I
is, "Thank you for going to work." I say this to
band every morning. Instead of just saying the ge
love you," it's affirming to say what I specifically
ate about him. With this statement I'm getting sp
love that he provides for our family. I love that he is
worker. I love that he is consistent and that he has in
And sometimes, I need to tell him these things speci

By elevating the conversation to this different
where again I'm inserting my values and emotions, I'n
telling him what I'm grateful for in detail. I'm showing
with my words what *I love you* means or what love feels
to me.

This concept can be applied to all of your import
relationships.

You can find ways to love the people around you
looking for the things that speak to them directly.

Instead of just saying, "I love you," find ways to te
them how or why you love them. Tell them specificall

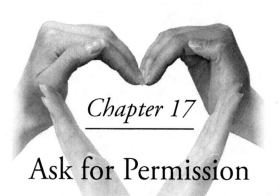

Chapter 17

Ask for Permission

Timing in communication is crucial to getting a positive result!

For example, children are notorious for being horrible at timing. Practically speaking, there's always a diaper blowout right before you need to leave the house, a pair of scissors that just happens to find its way into a child's hands the day before picture day, and a tantrum right before you're headed into a crowded store.

Sometimes, we become like children in our relationships and we're only tuned into our own needs and immediate feelings.

As a child grows into a teenager, they begin to see that timing is everything. If you've ever observed a teenager who understands this concept, it can be like watching a show about animals when the predator is hunting its prey. They wait and stalk (being helpful around the house), until just the right time (when their parents are in a good mood), and then they look for the perfect opportunity to "attack."

Sometimes their hunting techniques involve a divide and conquer strategy, where they look for the weaker parent and pick their prey off for ease and convenience. They know which parent is more likely to say yes to their question about borrowing the car, staying out past curfew, or going to hang out with a group of nondescript friends at an undisclosed location.

As much as we see these methods as obvious and manipulative, teens are learning a valuable lesson. They're learning to get what they want through behavior modification (even if that modification is only for five minutes) and timed communication.

Now, we think, as mature adults, that we're past this, but that's not true at all. Consider the last time you were around someone who wanted something from you. Odds are they were more helpful or maybe gave a compliment or even an unsolicited gesture of kindness before they approached the issue.

Most of us seem to have radar that goes off when people suddenly act like this. When this happens, most us of ask "What do you want this time?" and the game is up.

We think we're being so sneaky in our manipulation, even when the most unobservant person could figure out our motives. We're displaying a tactic of communication we hope works in our favor, even if it's blatantly obvious.

You can apply these same principles in your conversations. Not the hunter stalking the prey, or ridiculous brown-nosing, but the understanding that you're more likely to have a positive result if the person you're talking to is open and ready to communicate. This is where timing comes in.

You can set the stage, limit distractions, speak kindly, and then express what you like.

Ask the other person when the best timing for your conversation might be. Get permission from them, if possible, to approach the subject. Many times, the problem is not that we're unwilling to speak about a topic, but that the topic catches us off guard.

When we're caught off guard, a natural response is to shut down or put up protective barriers. Help others and yourself to avoid being caught off guard by planning important conversations in advance. You'll tend to get a better result in your communications.

In conflict, continuing a heated conversation where both people have dug in their heels is about as productive as reasoning with a two year old at bedtime by explaining the biological need for sleep as a basic human function. It's not going to work.

Try these tips for good timing:

* Wait until the person is not distracted and has had a moment to relax.

* Ask when the best time to approach the subject might be. Asking them for an appropriate time gives you permission to walk through the conversation with them, not drag them along. The best outcome

is when both people can start off agreeing on timing so they can come into a conversation feeling prepared.

- Neither of you should be tired, hungry or distracted with bodily needs. Making sure these needs are taken care of can drastically change the outcome of a conversation. If your basic needs are not being met, they will distract from your ability to have a complete conversation without a meltdown.

- ***Find time where you can be alone and uninterrupted.*** So many conversations turn sour because of the presence of others. It's always better to keep your relationship and conflict conversations only between the people directly involved.

These are some ways that you can start asking for permission for timing, scheduling, and limited distractions so your conversations can be more productive.

Avoid re-hashing the same thing over and over or just ending an argument instead of actually coming to a resolution where both people feel heard. Notice I did not say coming to a *solution*, but coming to a *resolution*. This means that, even if the conflict is not solved, there is a feeling that progress has been made and both parties feel comfortable waiting until the next conversation to continue.

In this search for good timing, ***look at the real reason you want to have the conversation.*** Is this something that needs to be solved right this moment? If immediacy is not required, then you want to wait for a better time to come back and discuss the issue under calmer or better circumstances.

Waiting often diffuses a situation as well just because time has elapsed. Often, in the moment, you may be heated or passionate, but the next day it's not even on your radar anymore. This is why timing is so critical.

You can ask directly for better timing for the best results. In asking for permission, you're also showing respect for another person, and their timing, space and needs.

> *"Wait for the wisest of all counselors, Time."*
>
> **Pericles**

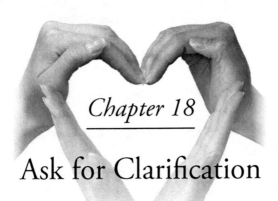

Chapter 18

Ask for Clarification

Clarity in communication is paramount to the success of a conversation. When you make assumptions instead of clarifying statements, you're asking for trouble. It's important to be ready to clarify the ideas of the other person when you enter a conversation. Making assumptions can kill a relationship if you're not careful.

When you make assumptions, you come at the world from your own limited perspective and often forget that it doesn't orbit around you or your feelings. You assume you know all of the information and that the other person is coming from the same perspective as you are.

At the risk of losing all credibility as an "elevated thinker," I want to share with you a story about my assumptions that my family will ensure I never live down.

When I was younger (not yesterday younger but maybe still too old for such a blunder), my brother came into the room and announced he wanted to be a garbage man. I immediately scoffed at him and thought to myself, "Well at least you'll have a job."

I was making pithy comments as only a sister can do when I was scolded by my mother and told to be supportive of my brother. She challenged me to be more positive and encouraging.

Being positive to my siblings was not my greatest strength as a child, but I wracked my brain for something that could be positive about working with garbage. In my naïve thinking and assumptions, I said, "Well, that's great, because if you have that job then you only work one day a week!"

For maybe the first and last time, everyone in my family was silent. I looked around the room annoyed that my "being positive" efforts were not being applauded. After the stunned silence, there was laughter as my family explained to me the error in my thinking.

You see, from my perspective, garbage was only picked up at my house once per week. I never understood garbage men worked all the time on a neighborhood schedule because my perspective was limited to just my world. My assumptions were challenged when I had to think about the logistics of all of the garbage in America being taken care of in one day.

I assumed my garbage was all that was important. I assumed what I saw going on in my life was true for everybody else.

Now try to do the relational switch on this concept. We often do this in life. We make assumptions that make us look very unintelligent based on our *limited* view of the world. I looked out of my house from my perspective and assumed that the rest of the world operated the same. I assumed that my garbage was all that mattered.

When you start to ask for clarification instead of just making assumptions, you go deeper in your relationships. You connect better and understand the perspective that others are coming from and not just your own.

Every stage of a relationship, whether it's new, fairly established, or long-term, could benefit from re-evaluating your assumptions.

When you're in a new situation—with a new person— you come to the table with your own judgments and assumptions about what that other person is like, what their experience may have been, and how well you're going to get along with them.

This is one area where if you stop and ask for clarification, instead of just making the assumption and sticking with it, you get to know people right away at a better level by asking for clarification and for their perspective.

This is also true for people who you've had some connection with, where you start to assume you know them. You can actually begin to ask again, "I think I know this about you, but tell me more," or, "Is this assumption correct?"

It's also a powerful tool in long-term relationships because, as you know, people change. Their interests and feelings change. This is revolutionary in long-term relationships.

You feel you have a good grasp on each other, but sometimes it's healthy to ask what may have changed. What is new that is shaping the worldview, passions or preferences of another person? You're not living life in a stagnant manner. The world is changing and so are the people in it. You're wise to be aware of these changes and be prepared to incorporate them into your understanding.

When you're brave enough to ask about those changes and challenge your preconceived assumptions, you're also able to bring the relationship to a more exciting conversational level.

When you feel like you've stopped connecting, it's a great time to start challenging assumptions.

Most of the time, when you're stuck in a rut, you think that you understand how you and the other person both feel and that nothing is going to change.

Instead of getting stuck in that rut and staying there, why not climb out? You can decide you're going to ask some intentional questions to see if your assumptions are still correct, to see if you're still using methods that are effective with that person or if you're still speaking in a way that reflects love or affection to them.

The first main benefit of having an assumption-challenging conversation will likely be that the other person is surprised. We tend to be creatures of habit, and when your routines are broken or challenged, you might get just the jolt you need to re-start your thinking.

Surprise is one of the ways you can redirect a conversation or someone's attitude toward you.

People will often be surprised you care enough to challenge your old assumptions or find out what their current feelings are versus simply continuing based upon what you thought you knew before.

Such a surprise can completely change the outcome of your conversations and your relationship. The other person can feel a rekindled love for you as well as a deeper connection, as they feel that you care and are interested.

Show you care by continuing to get to know those around you. Just as you learn and grow, others are also in the same process. It's wrong to assume that the path you walk is the same as another's.

Walk a mile in the other person's shoes or intentionally ask, "What is it like to be you?" This curiosity can spark new connection as people feel valued. Always be looking for ways to deepen, clarify, and re-shape your views so you're incorporating new information into your perspective.

"Be curious, not judgmental."

Walt Whitman

Part Three

Overcoming
Communication
Challenges

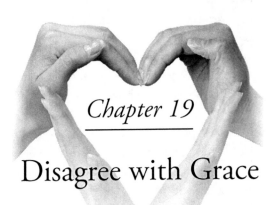

Chapter 19

Disagree with Grace

Plenty of times we end a conversation with a loved one or someone we're in a relationship with by saying, "Well, I guess we agree to disagree." Really what we're reiterating is the fact that we don't think *they're* correct in *their* assumptions.

As children, many of us understood that saying "I'm sorry" was very difficult because it meant admitting you had some responsibility in the relationship. Children see the world as "happening to them" and it is hard for them to understand their role in things.

Some of us are still stuck in this thinking as adults. We cannot disagree with someone without attacking his or her intelligence, character, or thinking.

Instead of attacking with this attitude, you can approach a conversation with grace and give some concessions. Although you might disagree with the conclusion the other person has come to, you can still find merit in how they arrived at their conclusion, *from their perspective.*

157

Facts and truth aren't relative, but how people perceive them changes based on perspective. You can honor the perspective of someone while not agreeing with their conclusion.

We see this in politicians. Often they don't listen to each other and they spew the same rhetoric over and over without making any real effort at seeing the other side. Most people have little respect for those in public office precisely because they are not willing to see or even entertain another point of view.

However, the best way to persuade someone is to look at the whole picture, not just aggressively hammer one point. I know that even when I disagree with someone, I have a basic level of respect for those who choose to look at life holistically. This does not mean that your actions or convictions will change as a result of looking at the other side of the argument. In fact, often my thinking is solidified when I have objectively looked at the other side of the coin.

Being willing to understand the point of another should not be a threat, but a practice consistently enjoyed for better relationships and a clearer understanding of the world around us. When you look at both sides of an argument, you can have an intelligent conversation and then draw honest, realistic conclusions.

An important note is that feelings are never right or wrong. They're just feelings. You have a choice about what to do with those feelings, but the feelings themselves are yours to hold.

This means that even if *you* think a person should not feel offended, sad, or angry, when they express these emotions to you, it's your job to acknowledge and accept their feelings. ***This single practice alone can change your communication!***

Earlier I mentioned that saying "I'm sorry" was difficult for many of us as children. In my experience, I had learned to say, "I'm sorry that *you feel* that way," which took all the responsibility off me and placed it on the wounded party. This was a horrible response.

I should have said, "I'm sorry that you heard what I said in a hurtful way. That was not my intention." There's a huge difference between these two statements.

It's hard to balance this concept, because there are two equally true points:

1. No one can *make* you feel a certain way.
2. Your actions *do* contribute to the way a person feels, reacts and processes a situation.

When you take responsibility for yourself as someone who has influence over the feelings of others, you then deepen your connection. Remember: we're created as connected beings and our words matter.

Some ways you can disagree gracefully are:

- Always begin with acknowledging and validating the person's path, experience, and conclusions.

- Find any similarities in their argument that you can agree on and share those similarities with them.

- Let them know you'll continue to think about their feelings related to the issue. This doesn't mean you'll change your mind, but that you'll think about their feelings and what they've expressed.

- Remind yourself: "I'm not going to continue to re-hash my point. I'm going to make my primary goal to show the other person I understand their position." ***This is a major key to disagreeing gracefully.*** When my goal is to show the other person that I heard their position, rather than to be right, I have elevated the conversation.

- Thank the other person for sharing and for their contribution. It's extremely difficult to be vulnerable and speak with someone you know doesn't agree with you, so thank them for that effort.

Disagreeing gracefully serves several purposes:

- It continues the conversation.
- It makes others feel heard.
- It makes you more responsible, intelligent and thoughtful.
- It gives others a reason to stop and consider your side of the argument and return the favor.

- ***It deepens relationships by validating each person and their experiences.***

When you disagree with others harshly, you put an end to the conversation and often end up looking closed-minded and foolish.

All of us come from different perspectives and have different ideas. If you can't reconcile those ideas and continue in a relationship, you're showing you're not emotionally mature enough to handle someone who doesn't agree with you.

You can be passionate about the things you believe in, like, or don't like. You may feel it's important to be right, to win, and to bring the other person to your side of understanding, because, to you, it seems like the logical conclusion.

Even when the issue is of extreme importance, remember the concept of timing. The person may not be ready to hear what you have to say.

Instead of seeing the conversation as a failure if you didn't convince the other person, learn to see it as planting seeds. Remember when we talked about relationships being like a garden? Each conversation is planting seeds or cultivating seeds that have been planted in the past.

We do not get the fruit that we want simply because we wish it into existence. It takes cultivation and care for things to grow. The same is true of relationships. Disagreement and conflict can be welcomed in relationships as part of the growth process. In trying to make things grow, sunny days are great but without the presence of rain nothing would flourish.

Apply that same thought to the people you disagree with. I would even be so bold as to say that if you have never disagreed with a person, you have not truly tested the roots of the relationship.

When you validate and acknowledge the other person—their path, experience, and conclusion—you then enter into a real conversation, not just a debate or argument. These conversations lead to trust. Over time trust builds relationships. It's relationships that change people's minds and hearts, not logical arguments.

> *"Don't flatter yourself that friendship authorizes you to say disagreeable things to your intimates. The nearer you come into relation with a person, the more necessary do tact and courtesy become. Except in cases of necessity, which are rare, leave your friend to learn unpleasant things from his enemies; they're ready enough to tell them."*
>
> **Oliver Wendell Holmes Sr.**

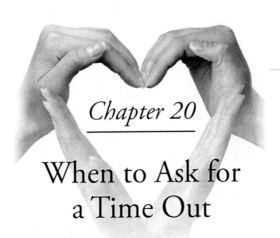

Chapter 20

When to Ask for a Time Out

E ven in early childhood, it's human nature to fight against some basic things that we need. How many times have you seen a child refuse a nap or have a potty accident because they were too wrapped up in playing? This happens because children are in a process of learning their limits.

As a child, these limits are often enforced by authority figures, but as an adult, it's your responsibility to be sensitive and attentive to these limits.

Now most of us would pay good money for a nap and I, for one, am proud to say that I am nearly potty trained. This concept of setting good limits to accommodate our needs goes much deeper than basic physical urges. Knowing your limits is part of learning to establish relational boundaries. You must know your strengths as well as your limitations if you want to be an effective communicator.

Knowing your limits will help cue you that it's time to take a break. This is a longer and more extended process than when you pause in a conversation. When you know that a time out is needed, you're asking to pull yourself out of the heat of the moment. You're asking for more than a few seconds to respond.

Taking a time out has an impact on both the outcome of your conversation and your mental well-being.

Unfortunately, I had to learn this the hard way (which seems to be my preferred method). I thought I was invincible and able to conquer anything at any time just with sheer will power. I saw taking a break as a sign of weakness and I refused to slow down for fear of missing out on something. This worked for some time until the cycle of natural consequences came around full circle.

With this thinking, I began to suffer from migraine-equivalent headaches, which came along with temporary paralysis of parts of my limbs. This would happen after any major event, whether it was happy, sad, or stressful. My body would literally shut down.

I would need to be in complete quiet and darkness to recover. Often, it would take up to a week for me to feel healed after one of these events because of the physical and emotional toll it took.

It became clear that stress was my trigger. I was not handling stress in an effective manner and it was manifesting in unpleasant and drastic ways. In barreling through life, I wasn't giving myself time to process, reflect or respond. I was taking in all the various stimuli and it was too much. I would push past the emotional, social and spiritual signs of fatigue and keep pushing myself.

As any fitness buff can tell you, sometimes it's okay to push through the pain, but you must know your limits. If you're a runner, you must work around the injuries you encounter and adjust your running accordingly. You can choose to go full steam ahead all of the time, but this method will only produce longer down times and less effective training.

It was through these times of physical incapability that I learned I needed to know my limits, to take a break, to step away, and to process.

Once I discovered this, I was better able to control my stress levels and response, even when I could not control the situation. I learned to take breaks. I learned to mentally prepare as big changes were coming. I learned to take things one step at a time.

This took time, but it allowed me to have less debilitating migraines as time went on. The migraines were obviously a manifestation of my stress. It was my body's way of making me slow down.

This concept can apply to life in general, as well as to specific conversations. ***If you're overly emotional or feel hurt, wounded, or out of control, take these as some major warning signs that you need to take a time out.***

If you understand that a conversation isn't going anywhere or you've given up that the conversation can have a peaceful conclusion, this is also a sign you need to take a time out. Your attitude directly influences how the conversation progresses and turns out in the end. If you've already checked out or felt hurt, it's going to be difficult for you to continue in a productive manner.

When you don't pause to take a time out, you're barging through the conversation like a sports team that refuses to take any of their allotted time outs.

A good coach understands that players need time to regroup and restructure their plan. They need encouragement and redirection. This is most effective during a time out. If all a coach does is yell instructions from the sidelines, he is setting up his team for failure. Fans and players alike would not applaud a coach for ignoring time outs because it's a necessary, built in, part of the game.

Likewise, you might feel reluctant to use time in ways that seem "unproductive." It may seem more productive to push through and finish a project, even knowing that the work is not your best. Visible productivity may stop when you take a time out, but the level of productivity and the results after a break can make all the difference in the overall outcome.

In the same way, it's easier to push through and finish a conversation, even if it's to your detriment, because that completion feels good. But this "completion" is actually a false and temporary feeling because, as you know, those conversations are the ones you have over and over again because the issues were never actually resolved.

When you don't stop and take time to sort out your emotions and thoughts, it can keep you from having an elevated or intelligent conversation.

When you do take a time out, you're able to come back refreshed and with a new perspective. Psychologically and physiologically, you're able to continue the conversation in a more effective manner.

Taking some time to reflect can change the direction of relationships and conversations. Just as a team after a time out has re-grouped and seen things from a "side lines" perspective and is then better prepared for the game, implementing these principles can help you be better prepared for life.

"Sometimes the most important thing in a whole day is the rest we take between two deep breaths."

Etty Hillesum

Chapter 21

Know When the Conversation Has Deteriorated

When a conversation has ended after spiraling out of control, you might sit in the destruction and wonder what happened. Luckily, there are skills that you can learn to ensure that you don't get to this point.

Sometimes it's hard to tell when you need to take a break from a conversation. This is especially true when you're used to functioning in unhealthy patterns of communication. Explore with me how to recognize when things are getting out of control.

Here are some key signs that the conversation has deteriorated:

- When you or the other person have gotten away from the original topic or problem. This is evident when you're way off topic or adding unneeded emotion to the conversation.

- If your voices are raised or your tone is hostile. This is a poor foundation to having a positive outcome where both people walk away as winners. Elevate the conversation, not the volume.

- If one or both of you is standing, when you started the conversation sitting. This is subtle but there can be a literal elevation in your body as you try to make a point or protect yourself.

- If there's hurtful or foul language being used.

- If you or the other person bring up unrelated issues from the past.

- If you have hot-button issues that have been pushed on either side with the aim to cause conflict.

- If you or the other person has shut down and stopped communicating. Sometimes the more dominant communicator may feel that when the other person is quiet, they're finally being heard. Often, the more introverted person has shut down emotionally and is no longer engaging in conversation at all. They're actually being quiet and hoping the dominant person will eventually run out of steam.

If any of these dilemmas arise, you can acknowledge the conversation has deteriorated and it's time to make a different choice about how to proceed.

Here are some tools to deal with a difficult person or conversation. This is a recap of what we have learned so far. You can start by stating what you want and need to do:

- I want to take control of what I can have control over. This goes back to the Hold and Fold principle. I want to take control of what I'm able to hold and I want to fold the rest.

- I want to pause, take a time out, or ask for permission. If that's not possible, I want to stop and listen intentionally to the emotion and values, not just the content.

- I need to know my own limits and pressure points and express these to the other person where appropriate.

- I need to know when to end the conversation. Not for the last word, but how to exit with a plan to continue later.

Saying, "I need to take a break. I want to hear what you have to say, but I'm angry so let's reconvene in 30 minutes," would be an example of how to use some of these tools once you know the conversation has fallen apart.

*If you allow a deteriorated conversation to continue,
it will not end well and both parties will probably walk
away hurt, which then maintains the negative cycle of
communication.*

When you allow a conversation to spiral out of control,
the attitude about the conversation and the person you're
trying to connect with is tarnished or damaged, and others
are less likely to be vulnerable the next time they're around
you for fear of getting hurt.

This can then taint how they come to the next exchange.
Have you ever had a conversation with a person that seems
like déjà vu? The same thing has played out again and again
and you know before you begin the conversation that it
will go nowhere? This comes from a place of informed experience, but it does not have to be the outcome.

The deterioration of a conversation works in a cycle,
and one person sets off this cycle. One person gives the
stimulus that creates the other person's need to respond,
and that response can be negative.

Then, the first person responds to that stimulus of negativity with negativity, and you just continue to go around
in that cycle.

*The deterioration cycle does start with one person,
but it's perpetuated by both.*

One obstacle in knowing the conversation has deteriorated is the desire to just finish the conversation and get it
over with.

Another obstacle can be when you don't realize that you're the aggressor and you're hurting the other person.

That's why it's important to look and see if the person you're communicating with has shut down or stopped communicating. Often this occurs when you get on a roll of emphatically explaining your point of view.

There are three main benefits to stopping a deteriorated conversation:

1. *Stopping a deteriorated conversation gives you peace of mind.* You know you're walking away from a conversation before you've hurt feelings or said things you can't take back.

2. You'll be able to come back to the conversation with a fresh slate and choose a new direction you'd like the conversation to go.

3. The other person will understand your care for their feelings outweighs the need to get the conversation over with or to be right. This builds trust.

Always make every effort to avoid letting your conversations get past the point of no return. Work to stop negative cycles and spiraling conversations in a timely manner and strengthen your relationships instead of weakening them.

Unfortunately, relationships with close family and friends are the ones where conversations deteriorate the most often and to the worst level.

We have the most conflict with those whom we love the most. For some reason, this seems to be a universal truth. We're hurt the most by the people we love. We also have a greater potential to hurt the people we love. Part of this is because there's a certain trust and vulnerability that already exists. You can express yourself more fully than you would with a co-worker or casual acquaintance.

To stop these cycles, go back to values and love. When you treat your loved ones poorly, you're reflecting the concept that you don't value them. You're sending the message that your communication skills, patience, and love are not to be wasted on them.

This happens in family dynamics often. Have you ever seen a coach, teacher or religious leader in action? They're great communicators and help others reach their goals. Sometimes, though, they've given so much that they're too drained to function at home. They may not spend time with their spouse, may neglect their children, and may blow off their friends. They don't lack passion, but they lack proper balance.

Protect those closest to you from your burnout. They deserve your love and attention. Invest in the people at home before you go out and try to change the world. Your home life reflects your true values and priorities. Remember, it's at home where you're closest to the "real you." Be willing to be the person that recognizes conversation deterioration. Do you like what you see? Does it match what you want the world to see?

"*Bad things cycle round and round. Those who were harmed seek to harm. Those who were blamed seek to blame. If we all choose to do otherwise, maybe someday it will stop.*"

Nina Berry, *Two and Twenty Dark Tales: Dark Retellings of Mother Goose Rhymes*

Chapter 22

Connect Without Needing to Win

Conflict resolution is an area of struggle for most people. My family was no exception. It was quite a challenge for my parents to tell who was right in each argument and who was wrong. It was also hard to decipher the truth from two conflicting stories of what had transpired.

Instead of choosing sides, my parents came up with an idea that was supposed to help us learn conflict resolution and honesty.

When we came to our parents with a tale of mistreatment from another sibling, it's not hard to imagine there were always two sides to the story. It usually went something like this "He pulled my hair!" Which was countered with, "No I didn't. She hit me!" Much to the annoyance of the adults, the only truth to be found was that there was a problem. Mostly, the problem was that, as siblings, it was impossible to admit fault.

My parents came up with the rule that we had to sit on the stairs with each other until our stories matched. Needless to say, we all spent much of our time away from school on the stairs.

As we sat on the stairs, we were supposed to decide and agree on which form of the story was most accurate. Both siblings were supposed to be responsible for what they had done and make the proper amends.

I do need to applaud my Mom and Dad for their creative thinking in this area. For the most part, this was a very effective way to get us to work out our own problems and disagreements. This was a great tactic for my siblings because they were learning integrity and honesty.

However, as the oldest child, I was using these "stair sessions" to hone my skills of manipulation. I completely missed the point of the exercise. I was supposed to be resolving conflict and mending relationships. Instead I was only concerned with my pride and winning.

To me, it was so important to be "right" that I didn't care how long I was on the stairs. ***My goal was not reconciliation, but winning.*** This worked for me only because none of my siblings were as stubborn as I was and they didn't want to spend their lives on the stairs.

Because I was more patient (or diabolical) than my siblings, they would come out saying, "I lied," or, "I didn't think about it the right way," and they would get in trouble and the torture of sitting on the stairs would end. I would come out looking like the responsible child while not taking any responsibility at all.

I knew that for my siblings it was more about taking responsibility and getting on with playing. For me, it was more about winning the argument. ***It was not until reflecting on this childhood memory as an adult that I realized the dysfunctional methods of my thinking.***

With my end goal always being winning, I might have had temporary victory. The real consequence, however, was disrespect from my siblings. They knew I would stay until I "won," so they would give in. This created animosity and distrust in our relationships. It also had a significant effect on what I considered important in a relationship or conflict. I was more concerned about how I was perceived by my parents than I was about truth. There was a huge discrepancy in values as I wanted to *look* responsible and trustworthy while my actions exhibited exactly the opposite characteristics.

Now that I'm older and not as sociopathic in my communication, I have learned a few things:

- That I could give up the need to be right in favor of building trust in a relationship
- The value of relationships over self-serving interests
- To take responsibility
- To listen and affirm a perspective that was different than mine

We might temporarily feel like we "win" a conversation, but we may have won the battle and lost the war. We lose the respect of people we're in communication with. We lose connection, trust, and empathy with them because they can tell we're just playing to win, not to connect.

We lose the ability to connect deeper the next time, and we lose the opportunity to continue developing a trusting, loving, open relationship.

In trying to win, we really come out losing.

When you take winning out of the equation, you gain a connection with the people you're trying to have a relationship with.

In a conversation, your first response, even when you don't agree with the other person, should be a statement of affirmation. Affirm their feelings or their thought process before you jump into your concerns. You can affirm their side of the story without injecting why you think their perspective is wrong. Simply listen and affirm.

You gain trust, loyalty, a deeper conversation, and new insights when you allow another person to feel safe communicating with you. They understand your communications are not a competition, but are communications between two equal parties who are *both* interested in the advancement of the other.

If you can change your thinking from a "me" and "them" paradigm, you can change your life. The people that you want connection with are always part of "we." When you grasp this, you understand that if both of you in the relationship don't win, no one wins. Winning only can be truly satisfying in a relationship if the win is shared with all parties involved.

Adding your own vulnerability or putting your own skin in the game can be helpful to you, making sure you're not just trying to win but that you're also trying to understand the perspective of the other person.

In showing respect and love for the one you're speaking to, you can understand their position, not just steamroll them into understanding yours.

Avoid these statements and behaviors to connect without needing to win:

- Statements that include "always" and "never"
- Statements that don't take into account the other person's feelings
- Cutting the other person off and interrupting in a way that sends a message you don't value their opinion
- Raising your tone or making the other person feel insignificant or less intelligent because of their difference of opinion

Are you sitting on the steps of your relationships and waiting for others to take responsibility?

> *"Winning is finding a solution both people feel good about. Winning is not compromise but a true sense of win-win."*
>
> **Gary Smalley,** *DNA of Relationships*

Chapter 23

Implement This Process in Small Daily Steps and Actions

I n any process, it's wise to pause and take inventory of your progress. When you're seeking to change your heart, mind, and life, it's easy to get overwhelmed.

Let's take a moment to evaluate what you've learned so far. It is important that you receive encouragement and guidance along the way as you seek to change. You wouldn't wait until your child was walking on their own all the time to praise their efforts. Each baby step can be celebrated and seen as a success. It's the same with the changes that you're making right now. Small steps can lead to massive action!

You've seen how listening is one of the key actions to putting all these communication skills into practice.

Notice that *listening* is an *action*. It's not something that can be done passively. Before you begin with your side of the conversation, listen for content and meaning to what the other person is trying to say.

Next, before you speak your views, acknowledge the views of the other person. *Show* them they're valuable to you—that you care about what they add to the conversation and the connection you share.

Finally, think about the values and feelings you want to express and ensure you express them. Go back to what you value and feel so you can send a clear message, versus being cryptic and unclear.

For your best results, start using these skills right away. This process develops and gets easier over time.

Your very next conversation would be the best time to implement these actions. Don't wait until you feel like you're an expert of these techniques or until you feel like it's the "right time." The right time is right now.

As you implement these steps, you'll notice a change in yourself and in your peace of mind about how you're communicating. You're going to be making fewer relational communication mistakes and having conversations that are more fulfilling.

You'll also notice a change in how others react to you. They'll see you've had a change of heart—a change in how you communicate—and that you have a genuine interest in them. This realization will help deepen their connection with you.

As with all these practices in relationships, there can be the challenge of people pushing back against your efforts to make a positive change.

It will take consistency on your part to show others that this is a lasting change, not just a ploy to connect with them momentarily. Don't be too quick to judge the hesitation of others. We're creatures that need to see proof before we're willing to accept things or change. This proof that others seek is only going to develop through your consistency over time.

New patterns have to be established, and that takes time. As with anything new, you'll need to take baby steps at first.

Take time to recognize the positive steps you're taking. These are the kinds of wins that will keep you moving forward while you become more familiar with the techniques. These wins won't happen overnight and they may not be evident when you first start out. Instead of looking at the end goal all the time, take some time to look at the ways you're making progress.

Ask yourself questions like:

- Am I being more authentic?
- Am I listening better?
- Am I thinking more before I speak?
- Am I being more intentional about my questions?
- Am I feeling more connected with others?

This is the best way to measure lasting progress because it helps you enjoy the process of change. If all you're doing is applying techniques, you're missing the point entirely. Lasting change comes from a change of heart, not just a change of practice. I encourage you to examine how your heart and mind can be transformed.

Are you working to:

- Listen because you care, not because you should?
- Speak intentionally with integrity?
- Have patience with people who are difficult?
- Change your focus from yourself to others?
- Empathize with people even when you don't agree?
- Ask questions and listen for the values of the other person?
- Know yourself and your values?

These are changes in the heart. These are the changes that last. Everyone is capable of behavior modification over the short term. Real transformation is much harder to find. Examine whether you're trying to make behavior modifications or if you're going all the way and letting this work transform your thinking.

> *"People say, 'What is the sense of our small effort?' They cannot see that we must lay one brick at a time, take one step at a time."*
>
> **Dorothy Day**

Chapter 24

Define Your Boundaries

B oundary issues are at the foundation of almost all of our relational turmoil. If everyone had healthy boundaries and respected the boundaries of others, there would be very few things left in life to cause conflict. In his book, *Boundaries: When to Say Yes, How to Say No to Take Control of Your Life*, Dr. Henry Cloud explores these concepts in depth in a way that helped to shape my thinking on this important issue. I want to share with you some of these concepts and how I have used them to change my thinking and relationships.

When you've established boundaries and are comfortable with enforcing them, you've mastered the biggest obstacle in healthy relationships.

What are your boundaries? It's important to understand yourself well enough to know when someone has crossed your boundaries, and then be brave enough to voice this.

For example, if you grew up in a family that was regularly yelling, as a result you may have established a healthy habit of not raising your voice unnecessarily. You may establish with people around you that if they choose to speak to you in a yelling tone, you will calmly let them know this is not acceptable to you and you'll need to excuse yourself from the conversation.

Handling situations like these is going to take practice. When you're establishing boundaries, it's natural for those around you to push those boundaries and see how solid or serious you are about your newly set rules.

Once you've established a boundary, it's crucial you stick to it and don't falter, especially early on.

It works best to establish boundaries around ways of communication, rather than issues or topics.

Avoid making certain topics off limits if you're trying to connect. Instead, design parameters around discussing those topics that work for everyone. In healthy relationships there are not topics that are off limits. Open and honest communication is a marker of health in a relationship. Of course there are topics that are harder to navigate well and this is where boundary application comes in handy.

Establishing boundaries comes down to being willing to put values in an order of priority that cannot be shifted around on a whim. For example, if you value your family and you've set proper boundaries, nothing will be allowed to come in and compromise your family connection. You will make choices with the well-being of your family in mind and you will say no to people and activities that work against the fulfillment of your family goals.

Boundaries are put up for protection of something. They clearly define what is important to you in a way that others can see. Cultivating boundaries is not only about keeping what is bad from coming in, but it's also about protecting what is inside the perimeter.

Using this process to set boundaries can strengthen your relationships:

1. **Recognize dysfunctional areas.** Most of the time, it's easy to identify areas of our lives where better boundaries would be beneficial. Look for the emotional exchanges that leave you feeling drained. Search for the situations where you often feel out of control or unheard. These areas are a great place to start when evaluating where new lines need to be drawn.

   If you notice that you and your spouse constantly fight in the car, it may be good to establish that conversations in the car cannot be about important or values-based issues. This boundary would be established after countless fights in the car where both parties come to understand the commute is not an effective place for good communication.

2. **Identify reasons for the disintegration that resulted in the need for setting better boundaries.** What is the dysfunction that made you decide boundaries should be applied? When things are going well, we don't feel

the need to place solid boundary lines because those boundaries are already being respected.

Maybe when you speak in the car, traffic and distractions cause one partner to feel overwhelmed. Maybe it's the confined space in the car that makes one partner feel trapped into the conversation without an escape. Whatever the reasoning behind the negative feelings, let those be known so the other person can understand the reason behind your boundary.

Once these boundaries have been established, it will take practice to create a new normal. You and others will have to watch for warning signs that the boundaries are about to be crossed.

3. **Stick to your new boundaries.** It's imperative to keep boundaries and remind the other person of your agreement. ***This can also diffuse an argument before it starts and allow both parties to feel heard and valued.***

Continuing with the car example, maybe you begin talking about your day in the car on the way home from work and then it escalates as you go into an issue about the kids or money.

When one communicator notices this, it's their responsibility to let the other person finish the thought and then remind them the topic is better discussed at home. Say something like, "That's a good point. We need to talk about that. I'd like to wait until we get home so I can give it the full attention it deserves."

Living a life without boundaries means you're living a life of chaos. When you allow others to dictate your life, you're not a victim, but a participant in your own destruction. Remember, as we established earlier, you're always making a choice. Sometimes you choose to let others impose things on you and sometimes you allow things into your life that are unhealthy.

It comes down to establishing boundaries and then making choices about what falls within those boundaries and what does not.

For example, during a sports game you might hear the home team assert "not in my house!" Of course, they don't actually live on the field or the court, but they take ownership of their playing ground and the rules and actions that will be accepted there. There is an established team culture that people are expected to respect.

It's the same when you establish boundaries in your life. You get to decide if an action is acceptable or if it needs to be met with a "not in my house" attitude.

Another important note about setting these boundaries is that you must apply the same standards across all aspects of your life. ***When you have some standards and behaviors that are allowed in certain areas of your life, but not in others, your life will tend to be out of balance.***

For instance, when talking about myself, I may say something jokingly that is unkind about my outward appearance. I know that I'm not the only woman who has ever struggled with this. I may think these words are jokes and they mean nothing.

Now let's take a moment to turn the tables. Let's say that even in jest someone said those exact unkind words to my daughter. You better believe I have a solid boundary around that taking place. I would instantly respond and the offending party would experience the wrath of momma bear!

Many of us operate this same way. We have stronger boundaries for the people we love than for ourselves. ***This inconsistency sends the wrong message.*** In fact, my negative words about myself may impact my daughter more than the joking of a stranger.

Make sure that as you establish your limits you do so with integrity and consistency to ensure balance.

You may be asking: how do we get to this point of boundary setting? You may already have great limits in place or there may be areas where your boundary lines need to be reestablished.

To check your progress regarding your boundaries, try these tips:

Ask yourself:

1. Have I worked through the process of defining my boundaries and understanding internally why they're important and non-negotiable?

2. Have I expressed my boundaries to the key people I interact with? This cannot be implied. This must actually be spelled out to others in a clear manner.

   The conversation might look like this: "I would love to help by being on that committee. I'm feeling crunched for time, and I want to make sure I have time for my family. How about I work on the planning parts with the group and leave the implementation to others?" This is an example of committing to something with boundaries. At times, the answer will just need to be "no" and that is acceptable as well.

   Delegate tasks that don't meet up with your values and learn to say "no" when it's appropriate. There is power in the word "no" that should not be underestimated.

   Another example of setting boundaries might go like this: "I'm trying to limit the negative things in my life right now. One of my negative habits is gossiping too much about others. I need to let you guys know that if the topic does shift to gossip, I will need to leave because I don't want to hear it or partake in it. This doesn't mean I'm judging anyone else. Can you help me try to break this habit? I'm working on being less critical and this would be so helpful, to wean that type of negative talk from my life." In this example you're setting up some clear guidelines:

* **A clear explanation of the reason behind the boundary.** It's best to phrase this in a way that isn't judgmental. In the example, the problem was with you and your need for change. There was no finger pointing at the rest of the group for being "gossipy."

* **A clear expectation of what will happen if the boundary is not respected.** This ensures people understand your actions when the boundary is crossed.

* **A clear outline of what you're trying to accomplish and what is no longer acceptable.** This leaves no room for argument. You set the boundary and so you set what is appropriate or not.

3. Are my boundaries being respected and am I following through with what I said I would do originally?

Follow through is critical when setting boundaries. When you don't follow through with a set boundary, you open the door for people to continually cross the line.

Have you ever heard a frazzled mom in the grocery store, threatening to take all of her child's toys away, promising an early bedtime, or swift removal from the store if she hears "one more whimper, whine, or complaint?" The mother is trying to draw healthy boundaries with her child that will teach him great life lessons. However, the connection falls apart when it comes to the follow through.

How many of us have heard parents say, "If you do that one more time . . . (Insert horrible, life altering punishment here)!"? The trouble is, they've said this a million times before and the child knows the boundary will not be enforced, so it doesn't need to be respected.

We can learn two things from this:

1. Avoid setting boundaries or saying that you'll do something unless you're ready to follow through 100 percent.

2. When you don't follow through, you give people permission to continue their actions and you're adding to their knowledge that you don't follow through with what you say.

As with everything, *it's important to find balance.* **Here are a few tips on how to balance boundaries with reality:**

1. Set reasonable and well thought-out boundaries.

2. Express those boundaries and their consequences clearly.
3. Follow through with the action you promised.

You'll find that people won't respect your boundaries if you don't enforce them. Some people will do whatever they can to excuse their behavior when they step over your boundary. These types of people are the most important to remain consistent with. They need to see that once you set a boundary it cannot be crossed without a consequence. The consequence might be less time spent with you, leaving a conversation, or you choosing not to take part in the dysfunction.

Some might think you're being judgmental as you set boundaries. Let them know you're not policing or judging them. You're only in control of yourself and what you expose yourself to.

It's self-control that you're looking for, not control of all the circumstances around you. To go one step further with this, it's a heart change that you're seeking, not just behavior change. This only happens with consistently applying your values to your boundaries.

Innately we understand this concept, although the biggest challenge is follow through. For example, when we come into the presence of an elderly person, we're more likely to adjust our language to a "G-rated" level. Even though these boundaries are implied and the elderly person might have the mouth of a sailor, most of us use discernment to negotiate the probable unsaid boundaries of those around us.

It's really just basic manners. ***Polite living has to do with making others around you feel at ease.*** Even the word civilization comes from the root word "civilis," which in Latin means civil. Being civil and living in civilization means there are some basic rules and standards that are held by all people. These standards don't guarantee people will agree with each other, or even like each other. The standards mean people will act in a polite manner.

If we can remember this, we will respect the boundaries of others and ask them to respect ours. This respect turns into trust, which can bloom into meaningful connections.

Challenges to Setting Boundaries

The most difficult obstacle to setting consistent boundaries is the people who will push those boundaries. They won't like that you've put any kind of restriction on your time, actions, or activities. They aren't comfortable respecting limits and it will take time for them to understand the seriousness of your new limits.

You might also begin to feel fear when expressing boundaries. "What if people don't like me anymore?" or "What if I offend someone?"

This can and will happen, so be prepared for the rejection and fall out that may come when you choose a healthier path. Surround yourself with those who will support your need for better boundaries.

Start with small boundaries and build to bigger ones. It can be dangerous to make tons of huge boundaries and announce your newfound rules to people in every circle of your life. Doing this can isolate you and make you less effective at enforcing the new boundaries. Make sure that you still have some people to fall back on for support. Take things slow and remember that one step at a time gets you to the finish line.

Also, as time goes on, you might become lax in enforcing your boundaries. It's so important to remain consistent with what you said you were going to do, so people understand the seriousness and integrity that your words express. ***To stay motivated to follow through with your boundaries, remind yourself of the original reason you created the boundary in the first place.***

Usually it's for healthier living, a more balanced life, more peace, less judgment, or a less critical attitude. There's something that caused you to say, "This is important enough not only to search myself to find out why I need a boundary, but also to put myself out there and tell others this is my boundary."

Also, when you've told others about your boundaries and you're not being consistent, they can be a built-in accountability partner to us as they say, "I thought you said you would leave the conversation," or, "I thought you said you were working on that." It can be a great way to keep us in check. The people in your support circle should be people that you know, love and trust. These people have your best interest, overall health and well-being in mind.

When you have consistent boundaries, you know absolutely where you end and another person begins. ***This means you can have total self-control.*** You can know who you are, what values you possess, and where you're trying to go in life.

When you've established and maintained boundaries, you get to live a more peaceful life. You get to live a life where you're safe and you choose how to react. In establishing these boundaries, you're making a declaration that you're not a victim of your circumstances.

Contrary to popular belief, it's the boundaries in life that provide us with the most freedom. See if you can work to change your thinking from a perspective that boundaries are just more pointless rules. It's the rules that keep things fun and safe. The rules give us a parameter for living that keeps things in balance.

We don't tell our children to stay in the yard to limit their fun and happiness. We tell them this because the street is dangerous and isn't a proper place to play. This boundary is for their protection and safety, not just an obscure rule. Many people choose to live life thinking they can ignore the boundaries placed by others, society or even the natural order of things, but sooner or later the error of their ways catches up to them.

You do have a choice in the matter. These boundaries are meant to guide and protect you, not to hinder and chain you. The sooner you can shift your thinking, the sooner you can live joyfully within your limits.

> *"Boundaries are to protect life,*
> *not to limit pleasures."*
>
> **Edwin Louis Cole**

Chapter 25

How To Respond
When You Get Hurt

F or most of us, it feels safer to ignore hurt and pain. We ignore things that hurt us physically and emotionally. You don't have to be a medical professional to understand that putting a Band-Aid on a broken arm or lying down to rest after extreme head trauma is not an appropriate reaction to the level of damage that has been done. We must learn to respond in a manner that is equal to the pain.

Even with the best of intentions, people will end up hurting you in life. This is part of living in the complexity of human relationships. Taking inventory and learning how to respond when you're hurt can help to elevate your connection with others and help solidify the responsibility you take for yourself.

When you're hurt by the communication of others, there are some steps you can take to work through your pain. I wish I could tell you that everyone who hurts you will have the desire and the skill to restore the relationship, but this is just not true. There are, however, some practical action steps you can take to move forward after you've been hurt.

It's tempting to sit around waiting for another person to apologize and make things right when they hurt you. However, when you realize some people aren't ready or equipped to accept the pain they've caused, then you understand an apology from them would be both empty and untruthful.

I can still hear the sarcastic voices of my siblings in my head when one of us injured the other. "Tell your sister you're sorry," my parents would say. "Sorry!" we would scream at each other, with disdain on our faces.

The sad thing is, many of us grew up doing the same thing and now we think this is an acceptable way to apologize. I know that my brother wasn't sorry for chasing me around the yard with a shovel or killing my favorite fish by giving them a cup of coffee "because they were thirsty." He was angry because he got caught and even angrier that he was being made to apologize.

In the grand scheme of things, many of us have been hurt much worse than just childhood mishaps. People may have used you, abused you, and damaged your life in unimaginable ways. That pain is real and it's important that you recognize what you've endured and the consequences of that pain.

True repentance and a real "I'm sorry," can only come from the other person seeing the hurt they caused and trying to reconnect the broken relationship.

Many of the people who have hurt us are not ready for this step. They're dysfunctional themselves and their pain is being passed onto others. This is not an excuse for them to inflict pain, but it's clear that restoring relationships and taking accountability is a difficult process for these people.

With this in mind, you can begin the healing process yourself with some practical self-care. This self-care depends on you and not on the person that hurt you. It has very little to do with raising your self esteem. The point is not to "esteem" yourself higher but to start *living* at a higher level. It has to do with seeing your innate value and caring for yourself in a loving manner. Your value as a person cannot be diminished because others fail to recognize your worth.

Follow these steps to go through this self-care process:

1. **Identify the wound.** What was said or done that hurt me?

2. **Identify the feelings it caused to come to the surface.** Was it shame, guilt, anger, hurt?

3. **Understand why the hurt affects you.** Ask yourself:

   * "Am I hurting because of what they said, or does it remind me of a past hurt?"

- "Is the issue really the issue?"
- "Was I feeling extra sensitive today when that happened?"
- "Do I feel the person is exhibiting how little they care about me with their words and action and that's why I'm hurt?"
- "Did the person hit on a trigger for me?"
- "Did the words of that person tap into a deeper fear?"

4. **Look at the behavior and the intention.** If I come to an event and I'm late, I usually excuse my behavior and understand that my intentions were good. Others see the bottom line behavior that I was late. This is such a valuable truth. Most of the time when we hurt others, we know in our hearts that was not our intention. *We all tend to look to our own intentions when we mess up, but when it comes to others, all we're willing to see is behavior.*

When others hurt us, we usually assume malicious intent that's not always there. When possible, give others the benefit of a doubt that they're stumbling along their own journey as well.

Reflect on the intentions of the other person as objectively as possible. Asking, "Was it their goal to harm me? Do they love me? Are they trying to tell me something valuable even if they said it in a hurtful manner?"

can be a helpful way to look at the behavior and intention.

5. **Go back to the concept of Hold and Fold.** "I hold only what I'm responsible for, and I fold the rest."

If I started a negative cycle of conversations that ended with me getting hurt, I need to first reconcile my responsibilities before I expect someone else should reconcile with me. This takes a deep level of maturity, and more importantly, it takes a commitment to the quality of our relationships.

When you're committed to connecting with someone, even after they hurt you, be willing to ask yourself the tough question: "Is this hurt or argument worth losing this relationship over?"

You might think this is a dramatic question to ask, but *hurt and arguments compounding one on top of the other cause marriages to turn into nasty divorces, friendships to end, and make strangers of people where loving relationships used to be.*

If, after every fight or argument, you're able to humble yourself, take responsibility for your role, and commit again to the health and longevity of the relationship, brokenness would be much less common.

Regardless of how someone hurt you, you get to choose if you let the cycle of pain continue. Try to fully understand the pain that was caused and what that pain can tell you about yourself. Don't waste your pain and hurt. Every time you're hurt, you can choose to learn from the experience. You can choose whether it strengthens you or breaks you.

Pain is an inevitable part of life that we seek to avoid. Embrace your pain as an opportunity for growth and change.

> *"Excellence is never an accident. It's always the result of high intention, sincere effort, and intelligent execution; it represents the wise choice of many alternatives—choice, not chance, determines your destiny."*
>
> **Aristotle**

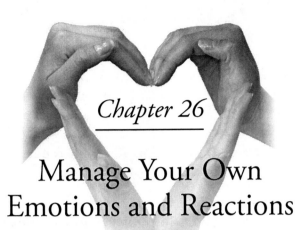

Chapter 26

Manage Your Own Emotions and Reactions

It's a universal truth that there are things we can control and things that are beyond our control.

Each person has his or her own issues and problems to bear in this life. The wonderful gift is that we can choose to let these issues define us or we can use them to our betterment.

I have struggled since I was young to stay physically healthy. As an adult, I've battled physical pain and chronic illness. In dealing with these challenges, I learned that ***taking control of my situation as much as I can is a key to finding peace in out-of-control situations.***

I've learned that even with an incurable chronic illness, I have some power over my outcomes. ***I'm not powerless in anything. My power comes from my reactions.***

As we deal with trials in life, we need to be mindful that: "I can only control myself, my actions, and my attitude."

I'm not suggesting I can cure a chronic illness with mind power or avoid a treatment like chemotherapy with a positive attitude alone. What I do know is that there are things within my control that contribute to my overall well-being.

To find peace in situations where life is out of control, I've learned two main lessons:

1. **I have responsibility for my actions and reactions.** I also hold responsibility for how I *view* my situation. Do I curl in a ball and cry "Why me?" or do I decide I want to explore all the things I can learn throughout my specific struggle? You might be amazed at the change that can come about in your life by elevating the questions you ask yourself. Instead of asking "Why me?" ask yourself "Where is the lesson in all of this?"

   I can commit to believing I will come out on the other side of my trial with a better outlook, more skills and closer relationships with those I love. I get to decide what to do in my circumstances. *My circumstances don't own me, nor do they define me.*

2. **To find peace, I have to let go of *everything* out of my control.** This includes how other people act, my external circumstances, and the attitudes of those around me. Letting go of the outcome seems counterintuitive, but it's actually more practical.

I can hold a burning coal in my hand and squeeze it with the intention of cooling it down. Even if in some small way I influenced the coal, I'm still left burned and scarred. It would be better for me to let the coal naturally smolder and cool. No matter how much I wish that I could bring the temperature of the coal down in my mind, it's not in my control. Outside sources could change the coal, but I don't have an impact. In hard circumstances, we to tend to hold tighter, trying to force the situation to change when the best results come from opening our hands and letting go. These open hands not only free us from the situation, but open us up to receive new things as well. A clenched fist doesn't let anything go but it also is not open to receiving anything either.

Willpower alone cannot change your circumstances. If willpower were the key, everyone would have vibrant health, wonderful relationships and successful lives.

When you take your troubled situation in stride and apply these two concepts, a few things happen:

- You can have peace in knowing you're doing all you can to grow and learn.

- You can have pride knowing that, despite the circumstances, you won't be defeated.

- You can know that you will be proud of the way you stood up under adversity and set an example for others.

- It can be difficult to bypass that primary reaction when something negative happens. It's natural to want to control our circumstances.

But when you can get to that deeper level of making a choice about how you're going to respond, you can experience the freedom that can be found in letting go.

For example, a woman could hope and pray all of her life that on her wedding day, rain would not come. However, unless the bride somehow creates a way to change the weather, all of her hoping and wishing are for nothing. She can choose to hope that everything is perfect, but it would be foolish for her not to have a Plan B.

She would have to release the outcome of the weather and focus her attention on the things within her control.

Imagine if you attended her outdoor wedding in the pouring rain and the bride insisted that she would get the rain under control. You would see her as absolutely foolish and wonder why she didn't take into account that rain might come and be ready to have the ceremony inside.

As her guests and bridal party stand in the soaking rain, do you think the bride would be getting much satisfaction out of the moment? Of course not!

You may think that example is extreme, but I ask you to think about worrying and fretting over the things that you cannot control. Even worse, think about the times when you may have demanded control over a situation that was impossible for you to regulate. We have all, at one time or another, looked like that foolish, drenched bride.

Go ahead and relinquish control. When you let it go, you can enjoy life instead of trying in vain to manipulate it.

Consider the ways that your circumstances and suffering have changed your life. Everything that is good and bad has the power to transform you, and you get to choose which direction that transformation takes.

"As my sufferings mounted I soon realized that there were two ways in which I could respond to my situation—either to react with bitterness or seek to transform the suffering into a creative force. I decided to follow the latter course."

Martin Luther King Jr.

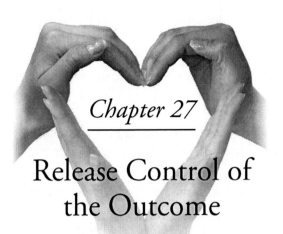

Chapter 27

Release Control of the Outcome

We spoke in the last chapter about letting go of the illusion of control. For example, the end result or the outcome of your relationship isn't always going to be what you planned.

Has this thought ever crossed your mind: "If people would just do as I say and let me run their lives, things would be so much nicer?" As much as this concept on the surface seems like a great solution, it's not effective.

Part of what makes relationships fulfilling is the fact that people choose to love us and invest their time in our lives. If free will was taken away, we would be robots with shallow and forced relationships. That isn't what we really want, although it's what we're asking for when we refuse to give up control of others.

This control is especially difficult to relinquish when it's control over a relationship or another person. The loss and changing of relationships in life is an inevitable reality. Grasping this concept and then dealing with the repercussions can be painful, but it allows for hope to come out of seemingly hopeless situations.

When others make poor choices, the last thing you want to do is watch them harm themselves. Although it's true that people need to explore their own path, it doesn't mean you have to walk it with them and watch them destroy themselves along the way.

This realization is also paired with the hope that, with unconditional love, people can change and their lives can be better as a result of their choices.

It can be very difficult to move forward after the loss of friendships or relationships of any kind. However, at times, you come to a place where *you may have to let people leave your life or be part of your life in a different capacity.*

This circumstance doesn't mean you need to cut people off if they're lacking, but that you explore the cost the relationship is having on your boundaries, values and life.

Instead of looking at every relationship as an ultimatum, go back to the concept of timing.

Some people are meant to be in your life for a certain amount of time. Sometimes people in your life have served their purpose and completed what they were supposed to do. You've learned the lessons you were supposed to learn from them and can release the outcome of that relationship.

This does not mean that we burn bridges with people, but that we go back to the concept of healthy boundaries. For example, I loved my Pediatrician as a child but there came a time when I needed to find a new doctor that could address my adult needs. As much as I enjoyed coloring in the waiting room and getting a sticker when I got a shot, that kind of treatment was only effective for a season in my life.

No relationship has been a waste of opportunity or time. Each and every person you encounter brings you the opportunity to teach them something and learn valuable lessons from them. Investing in others is never a waste of time or energy, though over time your investment level may need to change.

Asking yourself these questions can reveal whether you may need to make a change in a relationship:

- Do I value the person as an individual?
- Do I enjoy spending time with them?
- Do I respect this person?
- Is this person bringing valuable lessons into my life?
- Does this person make me feel safe and secure?
- Do I see the future "me" with the future "them?"

Your answers to these questions can help you to determine if it's time to shift a relationship. There will be times when relationships have run their course and become destructive. We need to be able to evaluate what to do when deeper and closer connection is unsafe or unwise.

Within this context, you have two main choices to make with the people you're considering disconnecting with:

1. **You can change the nature or intention of a relationship.** This could look like changing the expectations of this relationship, with the goal to change the outcome of the connection.

   Perhaps you're having an issue with a close friend. You love and care for them deeply, but for some reason they're no longer keeping your confidences when you share something about your life. You've addressed this issue over and over, but the trust is gone and there has not been any change.

   You don't want to completely cut this friend out of your life, but it would serve you much better to set boundaries and change the nature of the relationship. Instead of trying to *make* your friend become better at holding your confidences, you can decide you'll stop sharing such sensitive information with them. You may find non-essential things to talk about and find another person to share your confidences with.

   In this example, you're not kicking your friend to the curb. You're changing your commitment, your involvement, and your outlook on the relationship. You are only seeking to change yourself.

2. **You can know that a relationship is toxic and needs to be severed for the health of both parties.** This is a complete ending of the relationship. In this option, you end communication with the person and there's a natural grieving process that will come with the loss of the relationship. This type of relationship is detrimental to all involved and needs to be dissolved. This does not mean there are not valuable lessons to be learned from the experience, but that safe boundaries need to be drawn.

Option two is advisable mostly when abuse, extreme distress and problems of a recurring nature are evident and have not been resolved despite repeated attempts.

This situation is common with people who struggle with abuse and addiction in their lives. Enabling anyone, regardless of their struggle, is not loving them. To elevate the relationship with a person who struggles with these things means to allow them to take responsibility for their actions.

Even though the termination of relationships seems like a negative action, you can choose to elevate the conversation to be productive and not just hurtful or demeaning.

If you need to disconnect from a relationship completely, it's okay to tell the other person what you've appreciated about your relationship. This allows you and the other person to see the positive value that came from that relationship. You can also state your new boundaries and what is non-negotiable to you. These boundaries are based on you and your comfort level and not on the actions of another.

For example: "I have loved our time together and the connection that we shared. I'm feeling I need to respect your choice to drink and party more than I enjoy. For my life, I need to make the choice to step away from this life-style and from this relationship."

Again, here we're taking responsibility. ***We're not placing blame on the other person. We're only taking responsibility for ourselves.*** This is an elevated way to live and interact, even within the most dysfunctional relationships.

It can be very difficult for the other person when you choose to cut them completely out of your life. As mentioned before, there is loss that comes along with this and a grieving process.

The other person may not be ready to sever the relationship or may plead and beg to let it continue. That's why I suggest option one (changing the nature of the relationship) as the best way to start if possible.

When you go through any loss, it's important to first understand that it's a process. Changing or severing unhealthy relationships is a process, but it's worth undertaking to maintain consistency, integrity, and balance in our lives.

When you look at loss in relationship terms, there are so many different ways you can feel bereaved. You can feel the loss of a friendship or relationship. It could also have to do with the loss of what someone was to you or what someone should have been to you. You can mourn the loss of what could have been or the loss of how the other person contributed to your feelings. You will need to grieve the fact that the relationship will not be the same.

The grief process can take a long time and does require work, but you want to weigh the pros and cons and understand that ***loss and grief will not outweigh the peace from taking those toxic relationships out of your life.***

When it comes to releasing control of the outcome, it's important to remember that you're only in control of yourself, your actions, attitudes and responses.

Remember that the way the other person reacts to what you've decided or the boundaries you've set is their choice and not your responsibility.

Instead of staying inactive for fear of how the other person might react, it's healing to release the outcome of what is going to happen. Avoid imagining what the other person is going to say, how they're going to react, or the attitude they're going to have.

The outcome lies with the choices of the other person. This is what releasing the outcome is all about.

Remember to be safe in this process and use common sense. If you're faced with needing to remove an abuser from your life, do so with a trusted friend or in a controlled environment. Remain calm and take heart in the soul-searching work you did to be brave enough to make this relational transition.

By elevating your relationships, you're elevating your quality of life. The most powerful force as you elevate your relationships is the power of choice.

> *"You may not control all the events that happen to you, but you can decide not to be reduced by them."*
>
> **Maya Angelou,** *Letter to My Daughter*

Chapter 28

Who Can I Turn to When I Don't Know What to Do?

For your best relationship success, you must be able to balance the idea that you're independently responsible for your actions, but that your actions have an impact on others. When seeking this balance, it's helpful to learn where you need to reach out for help and where you need to take the reins.

There are things in life that are for us to carry alone and things we need others to help us carry. Knowing the difference has changed my life and my view of my struggles.

In the book, *Boundaries,* by Henry Cloud, the author presents a beautiful analogy that I would like to use to help paint a picture of balancing self-sufficiency and community.

A mentor of mine expanded on this idea, helping me understand the idea of balancing independence with relationships in the following manner. Let me share with you the insights I have gained that have helped me know when to reach out for help.

Rocks:

We each have backpacks of rocks that we carry on our own journey. Though it may be a heavy load, it's ours to carry. We need each other in so many ways, but there are also some things we can only accomplish by doing the work ourselves.

We must define what is ours to carry. To balance this perspective we also must know when to apply the principle of interdependence and how to ask for help.

I understand that I'm expected to carry my own backpack of rocks throughout life. Some of these rocks I choose, and some of these rocks are placed there because of circumstances.

When I know and accept my personal load, I have accountability for that load. I see that carrying these rocks is part of what is building up strength in me. I'm toning my emotional muscles as I carry this backpack through life.

If I'm constantly taking off the backpack, it means I'm expecting someone else to haul my load, and it also means I'm not developing the strength-training skills I need in order to navigate life well.

Boulders:

A boulder is something that completely overwhelms you. A boulder in your life obscures your view. This is something you cannot see beyond. You cannot see how to get around the boulder, and it's too heavy to move yourself.

Identifying boulders needs to be a daily practice. When something first hits us, we may see it as a boulder we cannot move. Often with time and tools, we come to see that our boulders can be broken down. Sometimes these boulders can be broken up and shouldered alone. Other times these boulders need to be carried with the help of others.

When a real boulder shows up in our path, we know we cannot handle it alone and it's time to call in the support team. These are the people we have identified to help us get through life.

Your supporters could be God, a spouse, mentor, best friend, or anyone else that's not afraid to help you with life's heavy burdens. These are the people who have committed to living out life with you. These are not "fair weather" friends, but people who are dedicated to seeing you succeed.

The first difficulty about calling in the support team is that you have to learn to *ask* for help. Being vulnerable and admitting we cannot do everything ourselves can be humbling and challenging for us. In asking for help, we're admitting that there are things we cannot do on our own. This speaks against what most of us are taught culturally and socially so it can be an especially difficult thing to do.

The second hardest part is letting go and actually allowing others to help. Letting someone assist you means admitting you're not going through life alone. It takes admitting weakness and relying on the strength of others at times.

Sometimes these boulders can be so overwhelming that we feel pinned down, like we cannot get out from under them. We need others to help us get to a place where we can plant our feet and see a way past the obstacle.

Remember there is no shame in needing support. The true shame would be in refusing to humble yourself to a level that allows others to come alongside you.

Even though the concept of personal responsibility applies to us, we need to recognize it's not all about us as individuals. Allowing others to enter into our lives means we let them see us even when we're vulnerable. This can be sobering for us and can be a gift for them as we allow their love to relieve and comfort us.

I have trouble asking for help because I can have an attitude of independence instead of interdependence. As I understand more and more the importance of community, my need for independence lessens. This is a messy process, but it has enabled me to enter into relationships that have substance and meaning.

These signs can signal that you need to ask for help:

* **People see your situation and they offer help.** Sometimes those around us see what we need more clearly than we do.

* **You may have stopped making progress in your challenge.** You feel stuck.

- **Your actions or attitudes are making things worse rather than better.** You might need to call in people to help you reframe and regain perspective of your circumstances.

One of the obstacles to reaching out for help is knowing who's actually there for you. We all understand the concept of a "fair weather" friend or somebody that's only around when things are good.

Look back on your life and the people who have been there when things weren't going well. These people have a knack for stepping in and helping in practical and loving ways. ***These are the people you want on your support team.*** These people deeply love and care for you and are willing to show that with their actions.

When you ask for support from the right people, you build better, stronger and deeper relationships with those people. You allow them to see into a deeper part of your life, to be a part of your pain and struggle, which connects them to you.

Trials and struggles, more than anything else, have been instrumental in solidifying my closest relationships. Good things connect us to each other, but tragedy seems to bond us in ways that are impossible to forget.

The people in my life that I've remained connected with are those who have shared in my pain. They're people whom I've held in their time of need.

These connections run deep and remain because it's with these people that I've weathered the storms of life and come out on the other side. They've seen me at my worst, and even with all of my baggage and scars, they choose to see me in the best light. This is a reflection of true support and love.

These types of relationships can go both ways. We may be building a valuable support team for ourselves, but on the flip side, we're building a valuable support team we can be part of for others as well.

What we're doing is starting a reciprocal cycle of supporting, loving, and assisting each other through life's struggles. This cycle continues to grow and nurture people in their time of need, which creates deeper relationships and more meaningful communication.

Try to identify your support team and those whom you can give support to. Begin putting into practice the concepts of interdependence and humility. Doing this changed me into a person who loves because of how much I have been loved.

I support others, not because I'm innately good, but because I know what it feels like to be broken, yet supported and loved. This support is an invaluable resource in life and in your search for relational growth.

"*Imagine how our own families, let alone the world, would change if we vowed to keep faith with one another, strengthen one another, look for and accentuate the virtues in one another, and speak graciously concerning one another. Imagine the cumulative effect if we treated each other with respect and acceptance, if we willingly provided support. Such interactions practiced on a small scale would surely have a rippling effect throughout our homes and communities and, eventually, society at large.*"

Gordon B. Hinckley, *Standing for Something: 10 Neglected Virtues That Will Heal Our Hearts and Homes*

Chapter 29

Assess the Damage You Have Caused

After having several vehicles of mine wrecked over the years, I have become accustomed to the process of filing an insurance claim. After the initial chaos is over and everyone is safe, there is an appraisal process to assess the damages that were caused.

The job of the appraiser is to assess if the damage is minimal or if the car should be classified as a "total loss." These assessments help in the management of a claim and they're needed to make sure that the customer can get back on the road safely, having made the proper repairs.

The same general process can be applied to relationships.

Even though you may be less eager to look at the issues that you're responsible for, we begin first with assessing the damage that you may have caused others because ***you're only in control of you.***

Some people can go through life imagining they haven't caused pain to anyone. These people are blind to the pain they've caused and often can only see the injustices that life has brought *their* way.

In moving to healing, it's important to first assess the damage you may have caused to others. This is not meant to lay a guilt trip on you, but to allow you to see yourself clearly before you ask for others to do the same. A humble heart first claims responsibility for its actions before it demands restitution for the times it has been wronged.

Part of being true to yourself is being able to be honest with yourself. This means making an honest assessment of your actions.

Think about the last time you looked at a picture of yourself. If you like the picture, it's most likely because the picture shows you in a flattering light. If the picture elicited a response of "Woof!" or "That looks nothing like me!" usually we request any evidence the picture ever existed be erased.

This attitude won't get you very far in relationships. That's why an honest assessment is crucial, even if you're not pleased with what you see.

Sometimes it's clear who you've hurt and sometimes it's more subtle. If you don't know that you've hurt someone, it's difficult to make amends.

Try these practical steps to move through this process:

1. **Without responding or excuse making, ask the other person what damage you may have caused.** This would involve going to the person, sitting down, and having a conversation with them about how you may have hurt them and then listening to their thoughts and feelings about how your words, actions, or attitudes impacted them.

2. **Pause to reflect.** Maybe even go away from the conversation and come back later. You want to actually think about what they said. *This step is paramount.* A quick "sorry" doesn't show you've connected with the other person or the pain you've caused. This surface level apology also doesn't allow for reconciliation, relational repair, or deeper conversation. Don't inflict more pain with a half-hearted apology!

3. **Respond to the needs of the other person.** Try to meet their needs. Perhaps they need an apology. Maybe there is some action you need to take to make things right. Find out what they might need from you for your relationship to be restored.

After assessing these questions, you have the choice of how you might like to move forward.

Sometimes we hurt others because we don't understand the importance of an issue to them. You might have values that aren't aligned or a lack of communication that is hindering you from connection.

It's wise to assess how another person feels and how you feel before jumping into an argument about the importance of an issue. The importance of an issue lies with the people involved.

For example, have you ever seen a child lose their mind because they were told "No?" Maybe they asked to go play outside or stay up late and to them it was the most important issue in the world. This doesn't mean a parent should give into a child's unhealthy behavior, but it's important to understand the level of hurt or frustration the other person might feel because of your actions.

It is not your job to rate the importance or impact of something for another person. Your job is to simply be able to recognize and acknowledge the importance of the issue.

In the above example, this might look like this: "I know that you were really looking forward to going outside and I can see that it was important to you to have time to play. We are going to have to do that at a different time, which I know is frustrating." Here the circumstances and the answer did not change, but the child was acknowledged and they knew that their feelings mattered to the adult.

You may be thinking, "What if the other person is exaggerating how much I hurt them?" or "What if the other person is making a big deal out of nothing?" Many times in relationships, you may disagree on the importance of an issue or a past hurt. You may see the problem as a non-issue while the other person is saying that they're deeply wounded.

Rating the Importance

In a disagreement, you may wish to rate what's important to each person. In a case where you don't feel the issue is important or you feel like the other person isn't taking the issue seriously enough, here is a way to gain clarity. Use this technique to try and enter into the perspective of another person. Practice the following scaling exercise to gain empathy for others, even when you feel the issue at hand is unimportant.

Imagine you have a scale that goes from one to ten. You're going to learn to rate the importance of an issue using this scale. If one is about as important to you as a petty nonissue and ten is about as important to you as the most highly held value you have, where does the issue fall in this scale?

Each party is expected to rate the issue. One person may think the hurt only registered at a two and the other person may feel the hurt is affecting them at a much higher number.

If the issue is a five or below for both parties, try to agree, apologize, and move on. This could be an argument about where to go for dinner, what the kids are wearing for picture day, or what time to leave the family gathering. Issues that are lower on the scale do not have deep values attached to them and they are not loaded with emotion. This is why an issue lower on the scale can be quickly resolved without the need for much conflict.

These are issues you might disagree about regularly, but have very little importance to the quality and health of your relationships.

Imagine arguing about where to go for dinner. This conflict could go on for half an hour and can leave both parties in a state of ravenous anger. If there was a rating system in place from the beginning, imagine how much simpler the process could be. "I wanted to go to the steak house and you wanted to go to the pasta place. We both rate it about a two on the level of importance. How about let's do pasta tonight and steak next time?"

Now everyone gets to eat and time was not wasted on petty arguing.

If you could stop in the middle of an argument and, right then, figure out a number to rate the importance of the issue, many issues could be resolved more effectively and without causing hurt or misunderstanding.

Agree ahead of time that a rating lower than five by both people isn't that important and can be decided by a rock, paper, scissors, or the issue can be dropped altogether.

If the issue is a five or above, even if this is for only one person in the conversation, it means there is some work to be done.

For example, when I'm speaking to a friend about the issue of being on time, my friend might rate the issue as a two, but to me it's a seven. This means we need to pause and talk about why the issue is so important to me, and acknowledge my feelings and values.

I may say "being on time to prearranged events tells me I'm important. It gives me a sense of security. It's also about my highly held value of respect."

Instead of my friend dismissing my feelings, they can enter into an understanding of the reason behind my high rating of the issue and can then acknowledge and affirm my feelings.

Oftentimes when I'm low on the scale of importance but someone explains why they're higher, I'm able to elevate my level of concern for the issue—not because I care more about the issue at hand, but because I care about the person I'm in a relationship with.

Again, it's important to note the value of timing. In the heat of the moment, you may ask me the importance of an issue and I could respond with a very emotional, "It's a ten for me, and we have to talk about it now!" This is not effective.

The point is for honest, objective communication about feelings, values and needs. This is not a tool for manipulation or a free pass to live in the extremes.

As you implement this technique, really think about your rating. Take a moment to think: "Will this still feel like such a high number in a day? What about a week? How about in the grand scheme of things?" Give your rating after you've calmly considered the issue.

This type of communication brings you into a place where you can hear and respond to the needs of the other person.

One of the reasons for this rating system is to see how situations may impact those around you. It can allow you to see what is important to others and it can give people a chance to let you know when something hurt or offended them. It can feel extremely vulnerable to admit that you've caused pain. It's difficult to admit the pain you've caused to another or to intentionally look at how deeply you could have hurt someone you love, because, in turn, it hurts you as well.

Try stepping into the shoes of the other person. It takes a great deal of honesty and self-examination to accept that you have the capability of deeply hurting another person. ***When you accept that fact and the responsibility for it, it's no longer about blame, but about healing and reconciling the relationship.*** It's no longer just about what you did, but how you can move forward and make it right. Making amends with others is a healing step. Listen to others as they rate the importance of an issue and listen as people rate the levels of pain that they may have felt. Then attempt to respond to their assessment of the situation with compassion instead of defensiveness. Issues big and small deserve your attention. When you give this selfless attention others can know that you are serious about creating safe communication.

As we have covered before, this is about heart change and not just behavior change. The guilt of your past actions can hold you back from a fulfilling relationship. Releasing this guilt and making things right (to the best of your ability) cleanses you and allows you to continue moving forward in this process. Assess the damage that you have caused so that you and others can heal.

> *"Chronic remorse, as all the moralists are agreed, is a most undesirable sentiment. If you have behaved badly, repent, make what amends you can and address yourself to the task of behaving better next time. On no account brood over your wrongdoing. Rolling in the muck is not the best way of getting clean."*
>
> **Aldous Huxley**, *Brave New World*

Chapter 30

Assess the Damage Others Have Caused You

Whan you assess the damage caused by the words of others, you remove the negative power those words possess in your life. After assessing the damage, you can then decide how you'll allow others to affect your life and view of yourself.

Just like the metaphor of the insurance appraiser, you must see fully the damage that was caused so you can repair the problem and get back on the road.

I can clearly remember the first deeply hurtful words said to me were in the first grade. I was on the school bus home and an older boy began using racial slurs and calling me names. I had no idea what the hurtful words meant, but the tone and inflection told me they were words meant to harm.

Many people have had a similar experience with early exposure to words that made a negative impact. The impact of personal choice is heavily emphasized in this book, but that needs to be balanced with understanding that things others say and do can have a profound effect on us.

The words of others can, indeed, hurt. As far too many of us know from replaying the negative things said to us, these words can have a lasting effect.

You can use the same steps used in assessing the damage you've caused to others to assess how you've been harmed through careless communication. **You can also turn these steps into a tool for healing when you've been hurt or offended:**

1. Ask what hurt or pain you've experienced from someone else.

2. Pause to reflect. Leave the conversation and come back later. Ask yourself, "What hurt me and why?"

3. You can and should respond to your need for healing. "Do I need reconciliation? Can I let this pain go? Have I forgiven the other person, or am I still harboring ill will towards them?"

Remember that in a disagreement, rate from one to ten how the disagreement or pain hurt you or how important it is to you. Then you can think, "How important is it now?" "How important was this pain to me at the time? *Try to honestly assess how the pain affected you in your life to help you gauge the proper response and action.*

When you're able to answer these questions honestly, you'll be able to break down barriers in your relationships that hold you back from true connection. This assessment transports communication to a higher level. It elevates the conversation so you're able to step into your own feelings and appreciate someone else's. ***In this way, you can see things from a true perspective and heal a relationship.***

We're meant to be in community and connection. We were not created to be solitary beings. Since nobody is perfect, life in community is messy and often hard to navigate.

When you enter into your own pain, you connect with yourself in an authentic way, and you can make some choices about how that pain or experience is going to affect you.

The same is true when connecting with others. When you're able to enter into the pain of another person, you're connecting at one of the deepest levels—the heart level—a vulnerable and beautiful level.

This kind of connection and relationship, where you're able to dig into past hurts and miscommunications, means you've significantly invested in the relationship. It means it's important enough to you and the person you're in a relationship with to join one another on this more vulnerable, raw level.

It also shows there is security and trust between the two of you, that you can get through these types of pain, and are willing to put in the intense work it takes to have a profound, connected relationship.

This is a process of fully understanding your past hurts and then choosing to release them for the sake of your own inner peace. Taking a close look at how you've been hurt might seem counterproductive to "moving forward." However, refraining from taking this time to discern the past takes away from the fullness that you can experience in your future.

"The present is what is happening when you strip away all the resentments of your past and all the worries you have about your future."

John Kuypers

Chapter 31

Let Forgiveness Free Your Conversations

B eing open to the process of forgiveness can breathe new life into your relationships. ***This is the ultimate way to elevate your conversations.*** Unresolved issues and anger weigh you down and make it impossible for your relationships and communication to soar to their highest potential.

It's possible to walk through life without forgiveness in your heart. Many people carry the heavy burden of grudges with them all of their lives. They pretend that harboring blame towards others doesn't hurt or hinder them in any way, but this is simply not possible.

Unresolved pain is a poison that seeps into all of the healthy relationships you're trying to establish. As you continue to strive for balance, please understand that unresolved hurt does not stay confined to the dark corners you may think it has been banished to. It will creep out in anger, addiction, miscommunication, and depression.

Let's take a moment to get real. How much you've been hurt in the past *does* affect your world view. Try to use the rating system again to look deeper into your pain and forgiveness to see how it might potentially be affecting you.

Use the one-to-ten rating system to ask yourself the importance of your past hurts. A rating of one suggests the pain is completely resolved and there's *no* bitterness left in your heart over the issue. A rating of ten suggests the pain of the past is choking the joy from the rest of your life. It consumes your thoughts and seems to dictate your actions.

Where do you fall on that scale?

There are some people who have done the soul searching work to honestly assess their life and say there's nothing unresolved that's holding them back. If these people were using the rating scale, they would put their problems and hurts on the lower end. This does not mean they were less hurt, but that the hurt is not having the same pointed impact on their daily lives.

For others, there are lots of unresolved issues that hold them back from trust, love and intimacy with others. If the unresolved pain is above a six or seven, it may be time to go through the process of evaluating whether the pain is keeping you from having meaningful connections.

Try to honestly and objectively assess your pain. Sometimes it's easy to let our history, prior annoyance, or past feelings compound until everything a person says becomes offensive to us. You may find there are lots of issues that have registered at a three or four level, but over time your overall rating with the pain in the relationship is an eight.

A higher overall rating comes from the compounding nature of not forgiving those who have hurt you. Tiny jabs and hurts can add up to some major dysfunction.

This is where we get into the delicate subject of forgiveness in relationships. Let's talk about some of the concepts related to forgiving another person.

First, as in many situations where pain is involved, *forgiveness is a process.* Saying you will forgive someone or even being willing to entertain the idea is actually the beginning of that process.

Do you believe these common forgiveness myths?

* **There are some things that cannot be forgiven.** This is simply not true. Not everything can be forgotten, but there is nothing that is beyond forgiveness, *if a person is willing to forgive.* Forgiveness is a choice to enter into a process.

* **Forgiveness starts with the other person being truly sorry.** Forgiveness starts with you. We will explore this more later, but forgiveness has very little to do with the other person.

* **Forgiveness is a one time decision and then I will forget.** Contrary to this myth, forgiveness is a

process and something that can be continually processed and renewed as you grow.

A mentor of mine taught me a wonderful lesson about forgiveness and gave some great steps that have helped me to understand the process of forgiveness and how to work through it. I want to share these insights with you in hopes that you can start the process of finding forgiveness in your life.

He first stated, ***"Forgiveness begins with an act of your will."*** Although you're wounded and in pain, you still have a choice of how you respond. This starting point is the beginning of your healing.

Pain is inevitable, but misery or dwelling in that pain is optional.

When you're ready to start the forgiveness process, there are some steps to work through. This process can be repeated at any time until the forgiveness becomes a reality in your life.

Keep in mind that saying you've forgiven someone (when you haven't) doesn't remove the toxicity of the grudge from your heart. Only a true forgiveness and heart change will release you.

Following these steps will allow you the reflection you need to start the process of being able to forgive someone:

1. **Give it a name.** What is the pain? What is the offense? Specifically name the hurt.

"You yelled at me and were acting aggressive and angry."

2. **Identify what you felt emotionally.** "Did it make me feel angry, unsafe, unloved?" This emotional reflection will support you in more fully understanding the repercussions of what happened.

> *"I felt unloved and unsafe when the yelling was happening. It made me feel powerless."*

3. **Identify who hurt or wounded you.** Name the person that inflicted the wound or the miscommunication. Be specific and purposeful in this step.

> *"The yelling came from my girlfriend."*

4. **Calculate your loss.** Understand, "How was I wounded? What was damaged? Was it my pride, my body, my sense of security, my world view?" Ask yourself what was lost or taken away.

> *"When she yelled, I did not feel like we had a reciprocal relationship. It wounded my pride and I felt like a child being punished."*

5. **Ask yourself: "How does this impact me?** How is this going to be lived out or how is this being lived out in my world right now?"

"I let this confrontation make me feel less trusting of other people and I allowed the hurt and fear to cause me to withdraw."

You may be thinking, "How will I know if I have actually forgiven someone?" Some people might say you've fully forgiven another person when you forget about the wrong they've done. I could not disagree more.

Part of the power of forgiveness is that you fully know and understand the hurt that was caused and ***you've made the choice to look beyond the pain.*** You can know this has actually happened when you have no ill will toward the person who hurt you and you have peace in the way you've moved on from the pain.

Forgiveness can only be granted by a person who is filled with love. The most beautiful example of forgiveness I've ever encountered is between a parent and a child. When a child disappoints or disobeys his parent, there is a breaking of trust and relationship. When the child asks the parent for forgiveness, although there may still be natural consequences, the parent is able to grant that forgiveness.

In no way does a parent love their child less because of their mistakes. A parent's hopes and dreams for his child's future are not tainted with memories of the pain, but instead, the parent is thrilled about the restoration of the relationship.

This is forgiveness in its truest form. Again, this does not come from the innate goodness of the parents or from the sincere apology of the child. The forgiveness being expressed is an extended expression of a deep and unconditional love.

How to start the process of forgiveness:

1. **Explore the full scope of pain.** Deal with the permanent and temporary repercussions of this pain.

2. **Lay down your right for vengeance.** True forgiveness means even if you had the chance to hurt the other person as much as they hurt you, you would not take it. *You decide the cycle of pain and loss ends with you and with your conscious choice to forgive.*

3. **Communicate to the other person what you're working on or have forgiven.** Release them, not necessarily from the consequence of their action, but from any ill intentions from you. This is the first step to working toward reconciliation.

This last step of actually talking to the person isn't necessary for the forgiveness process to happen. You can go through this process with someone who has died, someone you'll never see again, or someone who will never know how badly they've hurt you. *Forgiveness begins as a process of healing for you.*

Finding forgiveness does not mean that you lose your ability to keep yourself safe. Part of the forgiveness process is learning better discernment because of what happened. This is not victim blaming. Instead, it is victim empowerment. If I were constantly lied to by someone, I can forgive that person without blindly believing everything they say. I would have to exercise good discernment to know if I should trust the person again.

Forgiveness does not mean that you do not protect yourself from the offender, but that you gain a healthy perspective of what happened and what you will guard against in the future.

If I were crossing the street and was hit by a car, there are some things that I can learn from the experience. I should look before I enter the street. I should cross only at marked crosswalks. I should listen and look at my surroundings. I should wait until the path is safe. These are all things I could learn from the experience because these are things in my control. Again, this is not about blame but empowerment.

Many of us, instead of learning from the experience, choose to over generalize the negative to color the rest of our life. I could choose to be afraid of all cars. I could feel that no drivers are careful and therefore, no driver can be trusted. I can choose to never leave my home again for fear of being hurt again. This view of negative circumstance paralyzes and does not allow for forward growth.

Learn to balance forgiveness of others with a proper protection of yourself. Forgiving someone does not mean that what happened is okay, it simply means that regardless of the circumstances, your pain does not have to define the rest of your life.

Seeking Forgiveness

Granting forgiveness is difficult, but asking for forgiveness can be the most humbling experience for a person. When you realize you've hurt another person, it's important, as far as it's up to you, to reconcile.

Try these ways to ask others for forgiveness:

1. **Without excuse, name what you did wrong.** There is no defensiveness or explanation of behavior behind this, just a statement of what happened. You're acknowledging the pain you caused and taking full responsibility.

2. **Apologize for the hurt you've caused.** Ask the person if they could try to begin the process of forgiving you. Remember, this is a process for everyone, although the process always starts with a choice. Be ready to hear that the other person may not be ready to begin this process. You have the right to ask for forgiveness, but not the right to try and force someone else's process or timing.

3. **Work through reconciling with yourself for causing the pain.** Continue in a process of renewing yourself so you don't repeat the offense. Repentance means you understand the pain you've caused and you've modified your heart and behavior so you won't repeat the offense.

Being truly sorry means you've moved in the opposite direction of your hurtful actions. This change shows you understand your actions and their consequences.

For the other person, it also helps in their healing process to see you transform.

Some things to understand about forgiveness:

- Forgiveness begins with a choice.
- It doesn't condone the hurtful action of another person.
- It doesn't let injustice continue.
- It doesn't always involve the opportunity to reconcile.
- Forgiveness is not a process that should be rushed. For some, this will be a process that will have to be revisited again and again.

One of the greatest tools in being willing and able to forgive others is the grace I've been given by others when I've hurt them. When I understand the love that has been extended to me, it's easier to soften my heart toward others. I have discovered joy and peace when a relationship is reconciled.

Others have loved, forgiven, and accepted me, even with all of my flaws. This level of acceptance and love is extremely humbling. I see that, because of my gratitude for being released and forgiven, it's not acceptable for me to withhold that same forgiveness and reconciliation from others. I want others to experience the healing and joy I have been given through the experience of forgiveness.

> *"You will find that it's necessary to let things go; simply for the reason that they're heavy. So let them go, let go of them"*
>
> **C. JoyBell C.**

It's very difficult when the person you need to forgive or the person you're harboring resentment for has passed away or isn't part of your life any longer. It's important still to go through the process and that's why the third step of reconciliation doesn't necessarily need to happen with the other person.

If someone has passed away or is out of your life, you can still live out that restoration/reconciliation step in your actions.

You can write a letter, say a prayer, or let someone close to you know. Express the fact that you're working through this process of forgiveness with a person who's no longer here and understand you're working through the process of forgiveness for yourself.

The forgiving process is really for YOU. It doesn't have a whole lot to do with the other person. This process gives you peace and contentment and allows you to stop having those barriers around relationships that keep you from intimacy and connection.

Wouldn't you love to "get over" these issues that have you chained in destructive patterns and relationships? I use the words "get over" not in a trite manner that lessens the impact, but in a victorious manner. It's like looking down from the summit of a mountain and realizing all of the steps that it took to climb and overcome the mountain.

Once you get over the mountain, there is still a descent to be made, but the uphill battle is done.

How do I forgive, or get over, what someone said to me? Remember you can choose to be "OVER" it:

O: Offer condolences for your part (if any)
V: Verify the pain felt by each party
E: Eradicate the debt and your right to payment for it
R: Release the outcome

One of the things people frequently ask me is: "how do I get over what someone said to me? How do I get over how this person treated me?"

Using the acronym OVER is a great way to move forward:

1. **Offer condolences for your part of the conflict.** This means you're taking accountability for what *your* actions created in the relationship.

   This is the first step, because it's the only step that is completely dependent on you.

2. **Verify the pain felt by each party.** Listen fully to the pain the other person brought to you and that you may have brought to the other person.

   In a hurtful exchange, you can only experience your own pain, and you may not understand the pain you may have caused. This is a big step in forgiving someone when they've said or done something hurtful.

   Use empathy over judgment.

3. **Eradicate the debt and your right to payment for it.** Let go of the need to punish the one who hurt you, the need for their apology, or the need to get even with them, as you come to a place of peace—not with the action, but with your own heart.

4. **Release the outcome.** Whether or not the other person is sorry, or if they actually understand how much they hurt you, release the outcome and release them.

   The very first part of releasing the outcome is to understand that ***you don't control the life, action, or words of anybody but yourself.*** When you can fully embrace that concept, then you can embrace that you may never get the reconciliation you want. You may never get the apology you feel you deserve.

   Take heart even if the other person never understands the pain that they caused. You can still choose to move forward and feel peace. These steps enable you to experience real freedom from the hurtful things people say and no longer hold onto them in a way that damages you in moving forward in your life.

The process starts with you and is dependent upon you. This is a process the other person might not deserve, so it's extremely difficult to get to the point where you decide that you're going to release your desire to punish another person or see them suffer for the things they did.

When you do this, you're freeing yourself, not just the other person.

You're freeing yourself from the pain of re-living that negative conversation or negative action over and over. It's nice that the other person might feel forgiven, but again, they may not even agree they hurt you. This process is about the internal "housekeeping" that you need to do. It's not about cleaning up the mess of another person.

In this process, remember ***you have to continually release the outcome.*** Each time that conversation or person comes to your mind and there has not been reconciliation, it's important to go back to that same step and know that you've done, in integrity, what you could do and the other person's free will is still at play.

When you've fully explored what hurt you and why, and gone through this process (eradicated the debt and released the outcome), you've freed yourself to continue having good conversations, communications, and relationships with those around you.

The act of forgiving another person is actually a gift that you give yourself. The forgiveness you give has to do with *your* character, integrity, peace, and contentment.

True forgiveness isn't done in a condescending or manipulative manner. True forgiveness comes from a change of heart and thinking. The changes that occur can create blessings for you and those around you and allow you to live and love more fully. Start the process of forgiveness now and take hope in knowing that healing and peace can be yours.

Forgiveness is beautiful as it releases the chain of the one who gives it. Are you ready to be released?

> *Forgiveness is the fragrance that the violet sheds on the heel that has crushed it."*
>
> **Mark Twain**

Chapter 32

Learn to Be Wise Around Those Who Particularly Annoy You

I'm not particularly afraid of spiders, but I do find that if I spot one right before going to sleep and I'm not able to eliminate its presence from my room, I have an exponentially more difficult time sleeping peacefully. In this case something is literally "bugging me" and it can tend to consume my thoughts.

Unfortunately, people that "bug" me cannot be taken care of with a simple whack of a shoe . . . although this is tempting sometimes. I need to take appropriate measures to remedy the problem instead of turning directly to the extreme.

Sometimes, there are those around us that seem to annoy us only with their presence. Yet, we must put up with them in our daily lives.

To come to a better understanding of how we perceive these irritants, let's compare the experience to our skin:

We have an outer layer, the epidermis, which protects us from the elements. This protective layer is needed so we can get through life. We have all heard the term "tough skinned." This means someone is able to take critique or cruddy circumstances without it having a significant, stressful impact on their life.

The deeper layer of the skin, the dermis, is filled with connective tissue and provides more protection for our body. Within this layer, we find tiny nerve receptors that give us the sensations of heat, touch, and feeling. This deeper layer of skin is protected by the outer layer and it, in turn, protects the muscles, fat and tissue underneath.

These layers are needed for our safety. When something penetrates these layers, there is a wound and a healing process begins.

Most of us also understand what it means when someone gets "under your skin."

With certain people, it can feel like they're crawling around under your skin and annoying you from the inside out. For some reason, their actions or personality are just plain annoying.

There will always be certain people we will not like in this world. I know this may be shocking because *you* love and understand all people. That is wonderful for you, but I have not yet reached that level of maturity. There are just some people I don't like.

There are also certain people that don't like *us*. Another gasp from you just happened, I'm sure, because you're always so wonderful all the time.

These two truths are part of navigating life as an adult. So what can you do to transform these relationships into something more positive?

Positive Options

First, even if you don't like someone, treating them with disrespect only compounds the issue. Regardless of the reasons you don't like them, part of being a mature individual is learning to get along.

On another level, there are people you don't care for because of their negative and hurtful behavior. You can set appropriate boundaries with people who are destructive.

Think of the people that cause you major annoyance. If you can remove these people and their negativity from your life, ***go ahead and distance yourself kindly*** and move forward. I wish everything in life were this simple.

If you're like most people, keep reading because it may not be that easy. Such a person may be a close family member, boss, or casual friend that you cannot avoid spending some time with.

For example, your boss may not be open to a quick e-mail letting her know that you'll no longer be participating in life with her because of her negative attitude, rude comments, and lack of communication skills. In this case, you may be released from the negative boss and her attitude because you will also be released from your place of employment!

Since you cannot detach from every annoying person, you must learn to deal with them. Remember, even if someone is getting under your skin, ***it's your responsibility to decide how to react.***

It can be helpful to assess why some people irritate you while other's annoying traits seem to roll off you without consequence. Here are some concrete ways to identify if people have a surface level annoyance factor or if they're operating at a level you let affect you negatively.

How to know someone "got under your skin":

If the answers to the questions below are yes, take this as a warning sign to proceed with caution.

Use the acronym "SKIN" to ask yourself these questions in assessing the relationship:

- **S: Speak** to my sensitivities? Do this person's words or actions hurt me where I'm most sensitive?

  Did it speak to my sensitivities? Did what the person say trigger me, and is that one of the areas that hurts me most? We all have some areas where we're sensitive, and if someone speaks to those areas we can react very erratically and get hurt quickly. The other person may not understand why that area is so sensitive.

When they get under our skin, we need to remember to ask ourselves, how did that speak to my sensitivities or *how did that hurt me?*

- **K: Kill** the image of myself I'm working to create? Does this person make me feel devalued because of their comments or actions? Do they not value who I am or what I'm trying to accomplish in my life?

  Are they killing the image of me that I'm working to create? This is an issue, not just of pride, but also self-realization. Each of us is working toward an image of ourselves that's reflective of our values and character, and that's what we want the world to see.

  When someone annoys us or hurts us, it's often because they've damaged this image or not taken into account the image we're trying to create.

- **I: Injure** my pride? Do I allow this person to make me feel like I'm not worthy of something I desire?

  Did they injure my pride? Am I feeling hurt or devalued as a person as a result of what someone said to me?

  Did this person damage my ego or my projection of myself?

- **N: Nurture** bad self-perceptions? Is there some sliver of truth in the jabs that this person makes that brings me into a damaging view of myself?

  Did this nurture bad perceptions about me? Sometimes when something hurts, it's because there's a little bit of truth in it. We find that we may agree with the comment in some way and that doesn't settle well with us.

When you ask these questions, they can help you determine why the person bothers you so much or why the exchange was so negative for you. Ask these questions *first* instead of just chalking it up to the fact that the person isn't relatable, you don't like them, or you shouldn't be in a relationship with them.

You're taking responsibility for the feelings that their words may have caused to rise up within you.

When you know the "why," you can be extremely articulate when you come back to that person later. It can also help in your own progress toward healing and forgiveness.

You can say, "Your view of me is really not what I'm trying to create or what I'm trying to get across, and it upset me that you saw me in that light." Or, "What you said is something I work really hard on, and so I'm extremely sensitive in that area."

Assessing in this way gives you a starting point that's intentional and honest if you go to speak to the other person about hurting you.

Sometimes, you have to get to a point of maturity where you realize that the people that annoy you are probably not going to change. If you can come to this realization and move forward, it's even more advantageous for you.

Remember the young daughter-in-law that was constantly criticized by her in-laws? We came to the conclusion in that example that sometimes "You can't fix crazy." This may be the case with some people that annoy you.

Use these skills even if you don't plan on confronting the behavior. Even if you don't end up having a follow-up conversation after someone has gotten under your skin, you're better able to identify some of your triggers by using this process.

Then, each time those triggers are pushed, you can intentionally decide how to deal with them instead of just emotionally springing into action.

When you're unaware of yourself and your own feelings, it's not easy to listen to the feelings of others.

Also, it's harder to elevate your conversations because you stay on the surface level. Most of the time, the emotion that comes up to the surface is anger, and you stay mad and frustrated at someone.

If you sincerely find answers to these questions, you realize: "Am I actually hurt, embarrassed, or ashamed?" Those may be the underlying feelings behind your anger.

When you follow this process, you reframe the question or the whole conversation and go to a deeper level of understanding yourself. Then, you can move into a deeper level of communicating with others.

When someone gets under your skin, figuring out the reason can help elevate the connection when you come back to the issue later. It will also help in the development of your own understanding and relational growth.

You can also change your heart and perspective on the people that annoy you. Sometimes the irritation they bring into your life is there to sharpen and smooth you. As they "rub you the wrong way," you can learn to deal with life and people that challenge you. Sometimes it is exactly this friction that refines us into the people that we need to become.

It's in these challenges that you're taught patience, forgiveness, empathy, and persistence. You can even learn more about your own sensitivities and personality through dealing with difficult people. Embrace the difficult people in your life as having a purpose, even if that purpose is teaching you patience.

"Everything that irritates us about others can lead us to an understanding of ourselves."

C.G. Jung

Part Four

Going Beyond

Chapter 33

Looking Forward

Information for information's sake is pointless. I love learning and education but only because it allows me to *live* differently. The love of information should only be present because of our ability to apply it. I hold many advanced degrees, but as I have expressed to you in this book, I don't always practice common sense. Without common sense and application, the highest levels of education are practically useless. In the end, I see my degrees as very expensive pieces of paper if I have not impacted the lives around me with what I have learned.

Pairing education and common sense application together renders the growth potential in relationships and life limitless!

How Can I Continue to Grow These Skills?

As you begin to implement these concepts, try these practical ways to integrate your new skills into daily life:

* Teach these skills to others. One of the best tools I know for solidifying a concept is turning around and teaching it to others. It allows you to explore the subject fully and holds you to a level of accountability as you show others how you are applying the new concepts.

* Practice these skills with trusted people. Put what you have learned into practice. Just like any skill, the lack of use renders us less proficient over time. Practice doesn't ever make "perfect" but it can surely make "better!"

* Continue in self-reflection. Always remain ready to reevaluate yourself. As you grow and change, how you apply these concepts will grow and change with you.

* Revisit these concepts and exercises often. If I look in a mirror once before I leave the house, I know that I look decent walking out the door. If, however, throughout the day I never look at a mirror again, I may end the day with misplaced hair and food in my teeth. The same concept is true with life. We

need to reflect on ourselves and these processes often so that we don't forget them.

These skills are all part of a complex process of growth. This process cannot be learned or conquered overnight. Take the chapters of this book that stood out to you and start applying action to the concepts. Remember: learning without application is useless.

Who Can Help Hold Me Accountable?

Developing a support team is critical to your success. Go back and reassess, "Who are the people in my life who care for me, respect me, and can help me in my times of need?"

Choose people who are trustworthy, more mature than you, and can offer advice, wisdom and discernment when you need it.

This support team will hold you accountable as you start to make the changes outlined in this book and connect deeper with the people you love. They'll help keep you motivated, true to the boundaries you've set, and help remind you of the reasoning behind your deepened commitment to better relationships.

This support is critical to heart and mind change. Do not skip this step and think that you can go through life alone. Practice leaning on others and learn from them as you go through life together.

Who Can I Share These New Habits With?

Share your new skills and insights with your support team. If you're having trouble identifying who this support team might be, consider these:

- The people you teach or mentor
- Your friends
- A spouse
- A pastor
- Your children
- Co-workers
- Any trusted individual

I would suggest sharing these new habits with anybody you trust who will listen. One of the greatest motivators is getting the word out that you have decided to change.

Telling on Yourself

When you "tell" on yourself, the negative things in your heart are no longer secret, so they lose their power. Others see you even with your flaws and there is little room for shame and guilt.

Advancements in your new skills also have a chance to come to light and encourage others. Other people also have the opportunity to celebrate your success with you.

A popular trend in weight loss is putting up a "before" picture with a current weight and letting everyone see it before starting a weight loss plan. The point of this is not to bring embarrassment, but to add accountability and to say, "I don't want to be this person anymore." It's much more likely that people will be successful in their diet and fitness plan when they've let others know their intentions.

You can apply the same concept here. ***Let others know*** you're getting intentional about your relationships, elevating conversations, asking better questions, moving through past hurts and pains, and striving to have deep, meaningful conversations.

It's a lot easier to continue to be motivated and stay confident in your decision when you've let those around you know this is a critical part of your life right now.

What People in My Life Can I Apply These Principles with Next?

Whichever method of "getting in the pool" you decided to use in the beginning of this book, try to expand your practice with that method by identifying others that you can work to connect with. These could be people who were further down the priority list at the beginning, or people you never considered at that time.

Repeat this process with as many people as possible so it can become a natural part of your communication.

If you started with your spouse, move to your children. If you started with your mother, move to your siblings. If you started with your close friend, maybe you have other friendships that are worth deepening.

The first few relationships you tackle will be the most difficult because you're new to the process. Just like with anything else, it takes dedication and practice to strengthen your skills. Eventually, this can become a natural way to communicate and you can enjoy more meaningful relationships with everyone you love.

Elevation of relationships, effective questioning, and personal responsibility have the power to transform you as a communicator.

Keep in mind that having all of the techniques in the world won't do a thing if you're not willing to apply them. Focus on the long term, character, and heart changes that will make this process genuine and life-lasting. A true change of heart cannot be tainted by circumstances.

Let your heart and mind continue to develop as you work through this beautiful, chaotic, rewarding process called life.

> *"This life therefore is not righteousness, but growth in righteousness, not health, but healing, not being but becoming, not rest but exercise. We're not yet what we shall be, but we're growing toward it, the process is not yet finished, but it's going on, this is not the end, but it's the road. All does not yet gleam in glory, but all is being purified."*
>
> **Martin Luther**

Chapter 34

Celebrate Your Accomplishments!

Other than the fact that I like any reason to have a party, celebration in this process is a step that you must not forgo. Find ways to reward yourself for your work. Talk about your success with others and let them be proud of you while letting them be encouraged by your passion and growth.

Rewarding and recognizing your growth and achievements can keep you motivated! Keep up this important work and enjoy your relationships and conversations more with each step forward.

You might notice that people feel more drawn and connected to you because of your skills at helping them feel heard, loved and understood.

Let them in on the work you've been doing. Show them both the trials and triumphs you've experienced as you change your relationships. The whole of your experience, the good, the bad, and the embarrassing, could inspire someone else to strengthen themselves and their relationships as well.

You may never have understood this before, but your failures can be turned into successes. Every time you try and fail, you better understand the process of growth. In perseverance you can find the greatest joys.

Life isn't easy and relationships worth having don't come cheap.

- Be willing to pay the cost of having better relationships by being willing to fail.

- Be willing to say, "I'm sorry."

- ***Be willing to learn from entering fully into the process.*** Continue to better yourself and enrich your character regardless of circumstances.

This development of your heart and mind will never go to waste. Take some time to celebrate your failures, successes, and your process.

The culmination of your experiences and your attitude are what will dictate who you become. Let the person you're becoming be purposefully and genuinely constructed. When you have constructed your life with integrity, built and re-built, and found an unshakable foundation, there is no life storm you cannot weather.

"Success is not final, failure is not fatal: it's the courage to continue that counts."

Winston Churchill

Conclusion

As you come to a place of closure with this book, my hope for you is that you've been transformed. I hope you've gained practical implementation of common sense ideas and feel equipped to take positive action in your communications.

All of the growth and cultivation you've done is sure to produce wonderful fruit. The "garden" that you planted in the beginning of this process should be showing signs of growth that you can be proud of.

Let's take a moment to summarize some of the key processes that we've discussed in this book. This can help us to reflect on the processes, main points, and helpful insights that we gained.

In the Introduction of this book, we explored the importance of relationships and communication. We formed some idea of why change could be helpful and we were familiarized to some potential issues.

In Part One, we laid the groundwork for these important changes. You were asked to look deeper into your own story for insight. Looking at the past and the patterns that shaped current relationships was difficult and challenging work.

In Part Two, we studied how to elevate the conversation and our responses for better communication results. We evaluated values and emotions while changing how we ask questions.

In Part Three, we looked at how to overcome various communication challenges. This included learning limits, boundaries, and when to pause in a conversation. We explored the concept of forgiveness and letting go of the outcomes of our relationships.

In Part Four, we looked ahead to see how to continue to cultivate and grow these newfound skills while activating the power of relationships for accountability and encouragement.

This is a life-long process of assessment, growth, and reassessment. If you've gone through these processes and put some of these skills into action, these declarations should ring true for you:

- I'm more content with the way I'm communicating currently and I know I'm doing my part to create meaningful relationships.

- I can talk to others and model how I like to communicate with them.

- I know how to best give and receive love with the key people in my life.

- I understand the process of forgiveness and I can choose to enter into that journey.

- I can ask better questions that receive a more positive result.

- I can set boundaries that help me maintain a healthy life and healthy relationships.

- I can find peace in how I'm functioning in relationships.

- I can take full responsibility for my actions, without laying blame.

- I can allow other people to have the responsibility for their actions.

- I have the power to change my conversations.

With this book, you've been introduced to simple ways you can change your conversations to have more meaning and impact in your relationships. You can now choose to connect with others with truth and passion.

If you put these practices into action, even if no one in your life were willing to change with you, you can still experience immense joy and growth. You have the information to elevate your communications, questions and thinking when it comes to relational connection.

Overall, when you put these concepts into practice, you're working to change your communities from the inside out. ***The most impactful thing you can do to make a difference in the world starts in your own heart and mind.*** It's in taking responsibility and ownership of your life and relationships that you gain the ability to influence and encourage others to do the same.

Finally, I hope you've expanded your connections and experienced relational growth and change for the better. Continue to seek new opportunities to expand your knowledge and practice of these processes. With this expansion of self comes the ability to embrace more profound and meaningful relationships.

It's the desire of my heart that you see the depth of the impact you can offer the world. My hope is that you're encouraged, challenged, and changed by what you've read and that you're motivated to find points of application for these principles.

This process isn't about changing others, but reshaping our hearts to become a place where contentment is possible. We can learn to fully love and enjoy the relationships we've been blessed with to their utmost potential.

This depth of contentment isn't something that can be shaken or lost due to trials. When we understand others and ourselves, we open our lives up to the possibility of dynamic relationships that speak to our hearts, challenge our minds, and fill our souls.

> *"The happiness which brings enduring worth to life is not the superficial happiness that is dependent on circumstances. It's the happiness and contentment that fills the soul even in the midst of the most distressing circumstances and the most bitter environment. It's the kind of happiness that grins when things go wrong and smiles through the tears. The happiness for which our souls ache is one undisturbed by success or failure, one which will deeply root inside us and give us inward relaxation, peace, and contentment, no matter what the surface problems may be. That kind of happiness stands in need of no outward stimulus."*
>
> **Billy Graham**

What is Next?

If you're looking to move deeper into the material presented in this book, please visit us online at justlivingtoday.com where you can find workbooks and action sheets available for further growth and development.

If you feel you need more guided help in any of the areas discussed in this book, I would love to guide you as you put these processes into action. Connect with me online at justlivingtoday.com or on Facebook.

I would also love to hear from you via letter or email about how this book impacted your thinking.

Mailing Address:
133 Northeast 192nd Avenue
Portland, Oregon 97230

Email: coach@justlivingtoday.com
Website: www.justlivingtoday.com

Visit me online if you would like a complimentary coaching consultation to evaluate your relational and communication needs.

About the Author

Dr. Jessica Lynn Taylor, founder of Just Living Today, LLC, is a coach and counselor specializing in the areas of family and relationship development. Her passion is facilitating contentment and peace to families in crisis. She loves education and is always trying to discover practical, common sense ways to facilitate learning.

She holds a Master's degree from Liberty University in Human Services with an emphasis in Marriage and Family Studies, completed her Certified Professional Coaching training at The Center for Coach Training in 2009, and now uses her coaching skills to serve relationships in need. Jessica earned her Ph. D. in Christian Counseling from Northwestern Theological Seminary and plans to continue in family and relationship coaching.

Formal education aside, Jessica is the oldest of five children from a blended family that has given her life experience in countless realms of communication. Growing up, Jessica lived in both rural and urban settings throughout the state of Oregon. She is happily married to her devoted husband, and is settling into life as a mother with their new baby girl.

Jessica works as a relationship and family coach helping families to develop skills and tools for practical application. She loves working with youth and families and seeing the genuine transformations that happen when even one person in the family system is willing to implement small changes.

Jessica is the Director of Youth Ministry at a small church in Gresham, Oregon where she works with adolescent students in areas of spiritual growth, family, and life skills development.

As she continues on her own journey of growth, Jessica is deeply inspired by her relationship with God and her love of people. What was the inspiration behind this book? She says, "The youth and families that I work with every day have inspired to me write this book. The need for relational healing was apparent to me and spurred me to support others in discovering the joy they could find in deep, authentic relationships."

CPSIA information can be obtained
at www.ICGtesting.com
Printed in the USA
FFOW02n1352290114
3328FF